A779

D1180304

A guide to the
Pilgrims' Way
and North Downs Way

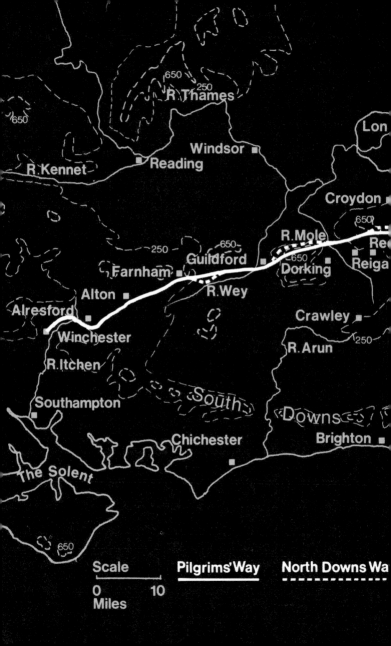

a guide to the

Pilgrims' Way

and North Downs Way

Christopher John Wright

R. Thames

R. Darent

Chatham

Downs

Rochester

R. Stour

Canterbury

Sandwich

650

250

Sevenoaks

Medway

Charing

250

Dover

R. Beult

Lympne

250

Folkestone

Weald

R. Rother

Hastings

Constable

First published 1971
by Constable & Company Ltd
10 Orange Street
London WC2H 7EG

© 1971 Christopher John Wright

Reprinted 1977

By the same author
'A guide to the Pennine Way'
'A guide to Offa's Dyke Path'

Designed by Ivor Kamlish MSIA

Printed in England by
W & J Mackay Limited, Chatham
by photo-litho

Contents

Illustrations

* asterisk denotes map (Ordnance Survey maps reproduced from scale 1 mile to 1 inch)

Acknowledgements

The author would like to thank the open-air organisations, fellow travellers, innkeepers, rectors and churchwardens and many others for their often unwitting help and guidance given whilst preparing this book, and for their valued criticism and support.

He would also like to thank Messrs Constable & Company Ltd, the publishers of Hilaire Belloc's 'The Old Road' and Robert Goodsall's 'Pilgrimage to Canterbury—A Progress Through Kent' for the valued permission to use material therefrom, particularly on those matters concerning the history and the characteristics of the route, as outlined in the preliminary chapters.

Aerial views are reproduced by kind permission of Aerofilms Ltd; the interior views of Winchester Cathedral by Pitkin Pictorials Ltd and of Canterbury Cathedral, A. W. Kerr Esq.

The maps in this guide are reproduced from the One Inch Seventh Series Ordnance Survey Maps with the sanction of the Controller of HM Stationery Office. Crown Copyright Reserved.

Introduction

Beyond the fringe of the sprawling suburbs of London's metropolis are many wild, unspoiled acres of pine and heather, fertile valleys and rich woodlands, but perhaps the best-known feature is the long chalk ridge of the North Downs, crossing the middle of the country from west to east, from Salisbury Plain to the Channel Coast.

The escarpment of the North Downs was from the earliest times an important link between the prehistoric settlements in Wiltshire and the Continent. Stretching in a great arc around the northern edge of the Weald the North Downs provided an almost continuous passageway for traffic. A trackway was made along the lower slopes of the escarpment when neither the Downs above, exposed to the elements, nor the vale below, with heavy clay soil and thick woods, were suitable for cross-country travellers.

The track long popularly regarded and now known as the Pilgrims' Way represents a large part of this route, and can still be clearly traced as it wanders through the green countryside from Winchester to Canterbury. The first authoritative account of the Pilgrims' Way was Hilaire Belloc's 'The Old Road' of 1904, by which time the 'pilgrim' myth and legend had become firmly established. Subsequent antiquaries and map-makers extended the application of pilgrim traditions, and the name found a place on Ordnance Survey maps which has been retained ever since. Belloc in his work was at great pains to build up the pilgrim aspect of this route between Winchester and Canterbury, but there is neither sufficient evidence to confirm or disprove its use to any degree of certainty.

Thomas Becket, Chancellor of England, had been elected Archbishop of Canterbury in 1162 by command of Henry II. Because he had excommunicated the King's followers, Becket was murdered in his cathedral eight years later on 29 December 1170, an event which altered the course of history in England. Henry had good reason to regret his hasty words 'Will no one rid me of this turbulent priest?' for the result was, ironically, the opposite of his intentions; the cause of friction between King and Archbishop had been Henry's determination to increase royal jurisdiction over the existing Laws and Courts of the Church, but this conflict was immediately resolved by the horror-stricken monarch yielding his ground.

The Shrine of Saint Thomas became a centre of medieval pilgrimage from all parts of Britain and Europe, and brought fame and prosperity to Canterbury. Because of the political history and other particular influences at that time Winchester was one of the principal starting-points for the religious pilgrimage to Canterbury, and the general or popular conception of the ancient trackway thus became established.

The pilgrimages reached their height towards the end of the fourteenth century, the period when Geoffrey Chaucer wrote his 'Canterbury Tales', one of the earliest and best-loved poetic works in the English language. The pilgrims whose progress is related by Chaucer followed another ancient route, the Roman Watling Street, which runs from London through Rochester and Canterbury to Dover. That particular journey started from the 'Tabard' in Southwark and seemed to have occupied the five days between 16 and 20 April 1386, a company of 'wel nyne and twenty', each pledged to tell two tales to while away the time on the long road to Canterbury.

Although the route followed by Chaucer was perhaps the most popular, it does not mean that there was little or no traffic on the North Downs route at the same time. Probably it was used extensively in both directions, for the ancient trackway was the obvious direct link for through traffic from east to west. Even as late as the seventeenth century this terraceway continued to be a useful road for those travellers wishing to avoid paying turnpike tolls.

Now for much of its route the Pilgrims' Way is forgotten by modern traffic. In places grassy track, at others metalled but quiet lanes, the Pilgrims' Way affords the cyclist and walker a chance to enjoy the countryside whilst following in the steps of history. There is a wealth of material to interest the traveller —prehistoric monuments, ancient castles and churches, ecclesiastical palaces and great houses, fascinating towns and beautiful villages. The features of natural beauty and the places of historic interest ensure an interesting tour for those who care for the past and for unspoiled countryside.

'Whan that Aprille with his shoures soote
The droughte of Marche hath perced to the roote, . . .
Than longen folk to goon on pilgrimages . . .
And specially, from every shires ende
Of Engelond, to Canterbury they wende,
The holy blisful martir for to seke
Than hem hath holpen, whan that they were seke.'

Brief history of the route

Six great ridges of high land radiate from the plateau of Salisbury Plain, and it is safe to assume that Avebury and Stonehenge drew the importance of their sites from this convergence: for these continuous high lands would present the first natural highways by which primitive people could gather from all parts of the island.

Radiating like the spokes of a wheel they are, clockwise:

1 The Cotswolds
2 The Berkshire Downs and Chilterns
3 The North Downs
4 The South Downs
5 The Dorset Downs
6 The Mendip Hills

From their heights even today will be seen the remains of woodland which made the valleys and the wealds originally far more difficult to traverse. By reason of greater dryness, ease of contours and height, the turf-covered ridges of chalk were an ideal original means of communication.

The North Downs had especial value in very early times, because Britain had similarities in religion, language and blood with the Continent. The passage westwards from the Straits of Dover to the centres of Hampshire and Wiltshire must have been by far the most important line of traffic in Britain, because:

i   The Straits of Dover are the natural entry into the country from the Continent.

ii   The Thames was the northern boundary of settled England until the coming of the Romans.

iii   The west of the island contained its principal supplies of minerals—tin, lead and iron.

iv   Southern England had the best cultivated land, the best climate and was in close touch with the civilisation of the Continent. Before the Industrial Revolution the centre of gravity of England lay south of the Thames.

The ridge of the North Downs is cut by five rivers—the Stour, Medway, Darent, Mole and Wey; it has moderately steep slopes to the south, is dry and chalky, bare of trees and not often indented by coombes or projecting spurs. The clean-cut embankment of chalk stretches for miles, along which man could hardly deviate, and led from the coast to Farnham. No definite ridge continues west of Farnham, but high rolling downs give good enough going along a watershed which avoided the crossing of rivers.

But if the ancient trackways led from the Straits of Dover to Stonehenge and beyond to Cornwall, why did Winchester come to absorb the traffic of the west and become the political centre of southern England, and why did Canterbury, an inland town, become the goal of this long journey?

The prevalent winds and tidal conditions of the Straits of Dover necessitated a multiplicity of harbours for the crossing from France. Persons embarking from Boulogne, Ambleteuse, Sangatte or Calais might at any time land at one of several points along the Kentish coast—Winchelsea, Rye, Lympne (Portus Lemanis), Dover, Richborough (Rutupiae), Ramsgate or Reculvers (Regulbium). These several points created Canterbury—an inland town for trade and defence, a point of concentration to the interior from the coast, and the town was established near to the tide, but without the loss of fresh water.

Caesar landed at Deal, but had to take the fort at Canterbury, and Augustine fixed the origins of Christianity in England here although he landed at Richborough. Thus Canterbury became the great nucleus of English worship and the origin, under Rome, of English discipline and unity in the faith for nearly seven hundred years. At last, influencing as much as influenced by the event, the murder of its great Archbishop in the later twelfth century lent it, for the next three hundred years, a position unique in Europe. Canterbury during those three hundred years was almost a sacred city.

As Canterbury was made by the peculiarity of the Straits and the confusing complexity of meeting tides, so Winchester was made by the peculiar conditions of the Channel. The Normandy peninsular jutting towards the Isle of Wight produced a crossing second only to the Straits. Although almost three times wider than the Straits, it has:

i   Protection for the estuaries of the Seine, Solent and Southampton Water.

ii   High hills inland as landmarks for navigation—St Catherine's Hill, 830 feet, and Barfleur Hill, 510 feet.

iii Refuges at Yarmouth, Newton, Cowes, and Ryde on the Isle of Wight, and Lymington, Beaulieu, Hamble, Portsmouth, Porchester, Langstone and Chichester on the mainland.

The submerged valley of Southampton Water continues inland to the valley of the Itchen, and the town of Winchester serves these Channel ports as Canterbury serves the Kent ports. The site of Winchester was central, it held the key to the only good middle passage the Channel afforded, and it was destined to become a capital.

A road must therefore have set out from Winchester to join the old east-west road from Stone-henge to Dover, and it would have led directly northwards towards Newbury. Later attempts were made at a short cut, to the east, and the Roman road to Silchester may have taken as its base some British track passing through Basingstoke. This was later superseded by a more direct route even further to the east, along the valleys of the Itchen and Wey, to join the original track at Farnham.

The old road then had Winchester for a new origin and Canterbury as a new goal. The neglected western end from Stonehenge to Farnham came to be called 'The Harrow Way', it fell into disuse and is now hardly to be recognised at all. Likewise the section of the Downs from the Stour to Folkestone became super-seded with the importance of Canterbury.

As Winchester began to assert itself as the centre of southern England—of open, cultivated, rich and populated England—the road grew in importance, the main artery between the west and the Straits. Thus Canterbury and Winchester, having so much in common, grew up over seven hundred years as the centres of English life—Winchester as a capital, and Canterbury as a ruler of religion.

The Romans in this frontier province set up their capital at York, but London, Winchester and Canter-bury were also great centres. One was the king's town, the other the primate's; the political and ecclesiastical capitals of the country. In the Dark Ages Winchester had its St Swithun, and in the Middle Ages Canterbury, with the murder of Becket, put out the light of Winchester and carried out the tradition of a shrine for continued pilgrimage.

Doubtless the road would have vanished com-pletely had it not been for one general and three particular influences, which, between them, have preserved a portion of it sufficient to serve as a basis for the exploration of the remainder:

1   Unlike the rest of the Roman empire, the British trackways survived and were not killed by the Roman roads. The political history of Britain at this period generally preserved antiquity.

2   The great pilgrimage to the shrine of St Thomas at Canterbury arose immediately after his murder in 1170. Helped by the Crusades between 1065 and 1292 to liberate the Holy Land from the Turks, the orders and appeals of a united church began to circulate throughout Christendom, men travelled and England became united. Henry II was perhaps the last king who thought of Winchester as his chief town; it was decaying and London more and more was becoming the capital of England. The roads from London to Southampton, Canterbury and the Channel ports would grow in importance, and the old road would decay. There was less traffic between west and east—the metals of Devon and Cornwall had lost their economic position and the iron of the Sussex Weald had taken their place. Winchester began to decline in importance. Then came the murder of Thomas Becket which brought to a head the quarrel between the Soul and the State. All the west suddenly began to stream to Canterbury, and Becket's tomb became, after Rome, the chief shrine in Christendom. St Thomas was murdered on the 29 December 1170, and for fifty years his feast had been kept on that day, but on the jubilee 7 July became the new and more convenient date upon which Canterbury was most sought. But the habit of such a journey had now grown so general that every season saw a pilgrimage. The pilgrims were compelled to take the old road because of its peculiar association of antiquity and religion, and the pilgrimage thus saved the road. But the pilgrims did not always follow the ancient way step by step. A prehistoric ford was lost in favour of a bridge or ferry, and sometimes the path was left to visit some notable shrine.

3 The establishment of the turnpike system in the eighteenth century perpetuated the use of the old road as the tolls chargeable upon these new and firm roads furnished a very powerful motive for drovers and pack riders to use an alternative route where such charges would not fall upon them. The Hog's Back summit road, for example, was a turnpike, but the old track lower down on the south side of the hill linking Seale and Puttenham was once more used as a way between Farnham and Guildford.

4 The existence of the chalk was a most important influence. It was never cultivated and therefore invited the wayfarer who was not permitted to trespass on tilled land, and a visible track was soon worn down by the feet and vehicles of travellers. There are many chalk pits on the hills and almost certainly their presence has been one of the reasons for the road's survival in later centuries. The chalk, as well as the resulting lime when it was burnt, had to be transported, and the old road provided the obvious east-west route. Some are of great age, and nature exerting her inexorable power has clothed them in a mantle of greenery so that they are barely noticed. These chalk pits generally lie on the left-hand side of the route when proceeding east because the Downs form the northern protection of the old road, and the quarry floors are at the same level as the trackway.

Route finding

The prehistoric route from Winchester to Canterbury is a distance of about 120 miles, a journey of some eight to eleven days. Finding the route is not always easy, even with the help of one-inch maps. The old road has been lost in many places and it is often difficult or impossible to locate it; it was not paved nor was it embanked. It has often disappeared from the clay, always from marshy soil, and only on the chalk has it preserved its unmistakable outline.

Modern highways and road improvements, and new intensive farming methods are together altering the face of the land faster than at any time since the war. The route has been obliterated in several places, and in others its line is purely conjectural, so that even eminent archaeologists differ in choosing the possible alternatives.

Just over 80 miles of the total length of the route are certain and fixed, but there are no great unbroken stretches between the lengths of existing road. No gap between the known lengths is greater than 7 miles, and some lengths of the road stretch 10, 13, and even 15 miles without a break. Between the lengths of known road it is reasonably easy to conjecture the 'probable' line of the remainder of the route.

The route has several principal characteristics:
1 The road never turns a sharp corner save to avoid a precipitous cliff face or sudden bend in a river. It

is not always straight like a Roman road, but it is always direct.

2 The road always keeps to the southern slope where it clings to the hills, and to the northern bank (i.e. southern slope) of a stream. The slope which faces south is drier.

There are four exceptions to this, but no stretch is longer than a mile in length:

Gatton, Arthur's Seat, Godmersham, Weston Wood.

In the case of the first three an excellent reason can at once be discovered: the road goes just north of the crest in order to avoid the long jutting-out spur with its re-entrant curve. This is because the re-entrant curve would be worse going, wetter, than even the short excursion to the north of the crest. In the fourth case there is no satisfactory explanation; the one true exception to the rule.

3 The road does not climb higher than it needs to. It flanks the ridge in several places, save for the obvious reasons:

a) To avoid too steep a slope for comfort.

b) To avoid the ins and outs presented by a number of projecting ridges—as at Colley Hill, Bletchingley and Boughton Aulph. Once on a ridge the road will continue, especially if advantage can be taken of a descending spur—as after Godmersham Park down to Chilham. The road would probably gain the slope and run along about 50-100 feet above the valley floor because of

i)   a better view of the way ahead;

ii) a better drained clay slope where the land would be drier than the clay of the lower levels;

iii) being above the margin of cultivation.

4 Wherever the road goes right up to the site of a church it passes upon the south side of that site.

(On its route the Way passes right up against thirteen existing or ruined churches—Kings Worthy, Itchen

Stoke, Bishops Sutton, Seale, Puttenham, St Martha's, Shere, Merstham, Titsey, Snodland, Burham, Boughton Aulph, and Chilham. In the case of eight of these it passes right up against the south porch, and in two (Bishops Sutton and Seale) it misses them by a few yards. St Martha's stands on the line exactly, whilst the route at Shere and Albury is doubtful.)

The road commonly goes north of a village and should, therefore, commonly go north of all churches. Indeed, it does pass many churches to the north, but it always leaves them to one side—as at Chevening, Lenham, Charing and the rest. It never goes close to their sites.

This rule is important when one considers the spot in which a church stands or has stood, and where, at the same time, the track is doubtful and has to be determined.

5 In crossing a river valley, the road makes invariably for the point where spurs of dry ground and rising ground come closest upon either side, and leave the narrowest gap of marshy land between. Primitive man would keep to a ford, seek shallow water, seek gravel rather than clay, pass as high up the river as possible, and keep to the general alignment of the track as much as possible.

The crossing of the Itchen, Wey, Mole and Darent give a clue to the important crossing of the Medway.

6 Where a hill must be taken, it is taken straight and by the shortest way to the summit, unless that road is too steep for easy going.

7 The road seeks the saddle of a watershed, if it be high, when passing from one valley to another.

Ivan D Margary in his 'Roman Ways in the Weald' sums up these characteristics as follows:

'The prehistoric route followed the main escarpment of the North Downs as closely as possible. In doing so it is in part a ridgeway, but it is also, for long distances, to be found as a terraceway near the foot of the steep escarpment, and, in some parts, both forms occur as alternative ways. The reasons for this are quite practical. Unlike the main ridge of the South Downs with its hard-turfed greenway right along the crest, the surface soil of the North Downs frequently takes the geological form known as 'clay-with-flints' overlaying the chalk. This sticky covering may make the going difficult in wet weather, especially just upon the flat crest of the ridge where the ridgeway would normally run. Again, the escarpment is sometimes complicated by re-entrant coombes and ridges which make it awkward for a direct track to maintain its position invariably upon or below the crest. Common sense indicated the best route, and this is why we find the Way now upon the ridge and now as a terrace below.

It is hoped that this guide book gives useful and detailed assistance in clearly defining the route on the map, though more waymarking is required on the ground. The Kent County Council is alone among the three counties through which the route runs— Hampshire, Surrey and Kent—in having erected occasional signposts, but unfortunately these are in places where they are really least needed and hardly ever where they would be most appreciated.

The modern pilgrim should be a dedicated footpath preservationist and carry pruning saw, shears and wire cutter, to deal suitably with the natural and man-made obstructions across his route. In high summer nettles, thistles, brambles, hawthorn, blackthorn and barbed wires are painful in their multitude. Modern farming policies have encouraged the use of portable, single-strand electric fences that can appear literally overnight and may be moved a few weeks later. Even the familiar line of a hedgerow can soon disappear.

Although the Pilgrims' Way has been specially surveyed for this book, these new and perennial hazards cannot be charted. Fortunately, their occurrence need rarely spoil the day's pleasure.

In general the Pilgrims' Way is a public highway, bridleway or footpath over which rights of way exist, but in places there is no public right of way, even where the route is distinctly clear. Care has been taken in the directions to make the route easy to follow.

The modern pilgrim will require the following sheets of the Ordnance Survey 1/50,000 scale maps: numbers 178, 179, 185, 186, 187, 188, and 189, but two-and-a-half inch maps will be better for most districts.

The maps in this book are at a scale of approximately one inch to one mile. The route described is marked therein by a broken line, whilst alternatives and diversions for better convenience and points of interest are marked by a dotted line.

On 16 July 1969 the Minister of Housing and Local Government announced his approval to a scheme put forward by the Countryside Commission for a long-distance footpath to be called the North Downs Way. This 141-mile long path will follow as far as possible the crest of the North Downs from Farnham, Surrey, to Dover, Kent, and will coincide in many places with the Pilgrims' Way.

Travelling for pleasure is best during the months of April, May or June, when the hotels, hostels and inns are less full and the roads not so congested. At these times the countryside is at its best; lovely stretches of remote and unspoiled track through deeply wooded shades and between growing hedgerows and banks bedecked with wild flowers. The North Downs are highly cultivated and heavily wooded, so that nowhere can one walk for long unhindered by plough and wire. Although every year the farmer ploughs yet higher upon their flanks, the Downs remain largely covered with thin, springy turf, sympathetic to walk upon. One may walk for miles without meeting a soul, unless it be some equally robust modern pilgrim, and from a hundred vantage-points see some of the most breathtaking views in southern England.

Transport facilities

When planning a tour of the Pilgrims' Way, ramblers often wish to know what transport is available to enable them to complete their programme in the time available.

As both Winchester and Canterbury and all points on the Pilgrims' Way between are within easy travelling distance from the centre of London, the modern pilgrim could easily set out from the city in the morning and return to his home in the evening, after having completed a 10-15 mile section of the journey during the day. By using a combination of rail and bus services the walker may return to the route each day, and save money and time in searching for overnight accommodation by sleeping in his own bed at night. Because the Pilgrims' Way is so easily accessible at reasonable cost by public transport, this feature will enable the route to be walked during days off and at weekends, summer or winter, by those who cannot afford a week or ten days off their annual holiday.

Motor bus services

There are four principal motor bus companies operating in parts of the Pilgrims' Way country;

1 Thames Valley & Aldershot
      Omnibus Co. Ltd
      (Alder Valley)
   Thorn Walk
   Reading RG1 7AX
   Tel. Reading 54046/7

   Serves
   north-east Hants
   and west Surrey

2 Maidstone & District Motor
      Services Ltd
   Knightrider House
   Knightrider Street
   Maidstone, Kent.
   Tel. Maidstone 52211

   Serves north and
   west Kent areas

3 East Kent Road Car Co. Ltd
   Station Road West
   Canterbury, Kent.
   Tel. Canterbury 66151

   Serves east Kent
   area

4 London Country Bus
      Services Ltd
   in association with the
   National Bus Company

   Serves London
   and the Home
   Counties

London Country Bus Services Ltd associated with the
National Bus Company serves London and the Home
Counties with express and country bus services:
a) Green Line Coaches are limited-stop buses and
provide luxury express travel to Guildford, Dorking,
Reigate, Redhill, Oxted, Westerham, Sevenoaks
and Wrotham.
b) Country Buses operate on all the above radial
routes but in a more leisurely manner and connect
with other satellite towns and rural villages. They are
integrated with the red Central Buses which cover all
main roads in central and suburban London.

Green Rover tickets cost 50p and may be used any day of the week for one day's unlimited travel on green Country Bus routes, but not Green Line Coach routes. Buy them from Country Bus conductors.

Golden Rover tickets cost £1.20 and may be used any day of the week for one day's unlimited travel on any London Country Bus or Green Line Coach. Buy them from the bus or coach.

Timetables and fares of Green Line Coaches run by London Country Bus Services Ltd are obtainable from London Country Bus Services Ltd, Bell Street, Reigate, Surrey, RH2 7LE. Tel. Reigate 42411.

Timetables of local Road and Rail services and other London Transport publications may be obtainable from London Transport, Publicity Manager, Griffith House, 280 Old Marylebone Road, London NW1.

Long-distance, limited-stop coach services are operated daily by Alder Valley, East Kent, Maidstone & District, Royal Blue and Southdown from Victoria Coach Station, Buckingham Palace Road, London SW1. Particulars of these and other services are given in the 'ABC Coach and Bus Guide' issued in April and October, which is obtainable from many bookstalls, or direct from the compilers, Thomas Skinner & Co. (Publishers) Ltd, 30 Finsbury Square, London EC2.

Rail services

The Southern Region of British Railways issue time-tables of their summer and winter passenger services in the region, and details may be obtained from:

    The Divisional Manager (South Western Division)
    British Railways Southern Region,
    Travel Facilities, Room 401,
    Waterloo Station
    London SE1.

The following types of tickets are available:

a) Day Excursion tickets are issued from the London terminal and suburban stations to the coastal resorts and other towns.

b) Runabout Rover tickets are available for unlimited travel in six areas of Southern Region for seven days between mid-March and early October from about £3.50 each. Unfortunately none of these areas conveniently extend over the North Downs area. However, a Southern Railrover ticket is issued from March to October for seven days' unlimited travel in the whole of Southern Region. Second Class tickets cost £17.50.

c) Special Ramblers' Excursion trains are run on alternate Sundays throughout the year. They start from one or the other of the London termini, and call at certain suburban stations in parts of the south-east counties, thus enabling walkers to reach interesting and out-of-the-way country at reasonable cost.

Leaflets giving particulars of these services and other concessions—cheap day returns, party travel, family travel, etc—may be obtained from the above address or any railway station. ABC publish a monthly rail guide of train services throughout Britain.

How to get there

The following list gives the main towns or villages on or near the Pilgrims' Way and how to get there by public transport from London.

The information is compiled from material supplied by British Rail, the National Bus Company and others. Whilst every care is taken to ensure accuracy the author and publishers cannot accept responsibility for errors or omissions or their consequences. Although the various companies represented make every effort to maintain their services as advertised, in the present financial climate, inflation and the withdrawal of rural bus services may not make this possible, and they reserve the right to alter or suspend them, or revise their fares, should the need arise to do so. The information given in this and the preceeding chapter may be altered at any time without notice, but the details given for selected principal services and fares are for general guidance.

ury | Train 21, 36, or 59 from Waterloo via Guildford from Victoria or London Bridge via Redhill
Country Bus 425 or 439 from Guildford or Dorking.

esford | Train 46 from Waterloo via Alton
Royal Blue from Victoria Coach Station
Alder Valley buses from Winchester.

on | Train 46 from Waterloo
Royal Blue (London-Bournemouth service) from V.C.S.
Southdown X16 (London-Gosport service) from V.C.S.
Alder Valley bus from Winchester.

ford | Train from Charing Cross, Waterloo, or Cannon Street, all via Tonbridge
East Kent (London-Dover service) from V.C.S.
East Kent (London-Folkestone service) from V.C.S.

esford | Train 25 from Charing Cross, Waterloo, Cannon Street or London Bridge.

tley | Train 46 or 57 from Waterloo
Southdown X16 (London-Gosport service) from V.C.S.

terbury | Train from Victoria, Charing Cross, Waterloo, Cannon Street or London Bridge, all via Faversham, and arrive Canterbury East
Train from Charing Cross, Waterloo or Cannon Street, all via Ashford, and arrive Canterbury West
East Kent M2, L1, L2, L6, L7, from V.C.S.

erham | Train 40 from Charing Cross, Waterloo, London Bridge or Victoria
Southdown X1, X3, from V.C.S.
Green Line 708 from Marble Arch, Hyde Park Corner or V.C.S.
Green Line 709 from Baker Street, Oxford Circus or Trafalgar Sq.

Charing	Train 18 from Victoria via Maidstone East Maidstone & District E1, E2, E3, from V.C.S. East Kent L2, L6, L7, from V.C.S.
Chilham	Train 18 from Charing Cross, Waterloo or Cannon Street, all via Ashford East Kent L2, L6, L7, from V.C.S.
Chilworth	Train 21, 36, 59, from Waterloo via Guildford Train from Victoria or London Bridge via Redhill Country Bus 425 or 439 from Guildford or Dorking.
Compton	Train 57 from Waterloo to Farnham, then bus Train 44 from Waterloo to Guildford, then bus Alder Valley 65, 66 from Guildford (Mondays & Saturdays only).

Dorking	Train 36, 59, from Waterloo
	Train 31 from London Bridge or Victoria
	Green Line 703 from Baker Street or V.C.S.
	Green Line 714 from Kings Cross, Marble Arch
	    or Oxford Circus
	Southdown (London-Bognor Regis service) from
	    V.C.S.

Farnham	Train 57 from Waterloo
	Train 57 from Winchester
	Southdown X16 (London-Gosport service) from
	    V.C.S.
	Royal Blue (London-Bournemouth service) from
	    V.C.S.
	Alder Valley from V.C.S.
	Alder Valley from Winchester.

Four Marks	Train 46 from Waterloo Train 46 from Winchester Royal Blue (London-Bournemouth service) from V.C.S.

..dstone	Train 40 from Victoria or London Bridge
	Green Line 708 from Marble Arch, Hyde Park Corner or V.C.S.
	Green Line 709 from Baker Street, Oxford Circus or Trafalgar Sq.
	Southdown X1, X3, from V.C.S.
..mshall	Train 21, 36, 59, from Waterloo, Victoria or London Bridge, all via Dorking
	Train from Victoria or London Bridge via Redhill
	Country Bus 425 or 439 from Dorking or Guildford.
..ildford	Train 44 from Waterloo
	Southdown X15 (London-Bognor Regis service) from V.C.S.
	Royal Blue (London-Bournemouth service) from V.C.S.
	Green Line 715 or 715a from Marble Arch or Oxford Circus.
..rietsham	Train 18 from Victoria, Holborn Viaduct or Blackfriars, via Maidstone East
	Maidstone & District E1, E2, E3, from V.C.S.
..lingbourne	Train 18 from Victoria, Holborn Viaduct or Blackfriars, via Maidstone East
	Maidstone & District E1, E2, E3, from V.C.S.
..hen Abbas	Train 46 from Waterloo, via Alton
	Royal Blue (London-Bournemouth service) from V.C.S.
..msing	Train 27 from Victoria, Holborn Viaduct or Blackfriars
	Country Bus 421 from Sevenoaks.
..ham	Train 18 from Victoria, Holborn Viaduct or Blackfriars
	East Kent L2 from V.C.S.
	Maidstone & District E1, E2, E3, from V.C.S.
..idstone	Train 18 from Victoria, Holborn Viaduct or Blackfriars
	Maidstone & District E1, E2, E3, from V.C.S.

Merstham	Train 30 from Victoria or London Bridge Southdown X2, X4, from V.C.S. Country Bus 414 from Redhill or Reigate Country Bus 440 from Caterham.
Otford	Train 27 from Victoria, Holborn Viaduct or Blackfriars Country Bus 401, 404, 421, from Sevenoaks.
Oxted	Train from Victoria or London Bridge Country Bus 410 from Godstone or Westerham.
Puttenham	Train 44, 57, from Waterloo to Farnham, then bus Alder Valley 65, 66, from Guildford (Mondays & Saturdays only).
Redhill	Train 30 from Victoria or London Bridge Southdown X2, X4, from V.C.S.

Reigate	Train 21, 36, 59, from Waterloo, Victoria or London
	    Bridge
	Southdown X2, X4, from V.C.S.
	Green Line 711 from Baker Street, Oxford Circus
	    or Trafalgar Sq.

Ropley	Train 46 from Waterloo via Alton Royal Blue (London-Bournemouth service) from V.C.S.

Sevenoaks	Train from Charing Cross, Waterloo, Cannon Street
	    or London Bridge
	Train from Victoria, Holborn Viaduct, or Blackfriars,
	    via Orpington
	Train from Victoria, Holborn Viaduct, or Blackfriars,
	    via Swanley.
	Maidstone & District E4 from V.C.S.
	Green Line 704, 705 from Hyde Park Corner or
	    V.C.S.

Shalford	Train 21, 36, 59, from Waterloo via Guildford Train from Victoria or London Bridge, via Redhill Country Bus 425 or 439 from Guildford or Dorking.

e	Train 21, 36, 59, from Waterloo, Victoria or London Bridge, all via Dorking
	Train from Victoria or London Bridge, via Redhill
	Country Bus 425 or 439 from Dorking or Guildford.

| dland | Train 25 from Charing Cross, Waterloo, Cannon Street or London Bridge. |

terham	Train from Victoria or London Bridge to Oxted, then bus
	Train from Charing Cross, Waterloo, Cannon Street or London Bridge, to Sevenoaks, then bus
	Green Line 705 from Hyde Park Corner or V.C.S.
	Green Line 706 from Marble Arch, Hyde Park Corner, or V.C.S.

| t Humble | Train 21 from Waterloo, Victoria or London Bridge |
| | Country Bus 470 from Dorking. |

| chester | Train 46 from Victoria |
| | Royal Blue (London-Bournemouth service) from V.C.S. |

tham	Train 27 from Victoria, Holborn Viaduct or Blackfriars
	Maidstone & District E1, E2, E3, from V.C.S.
	Green Line 719 from Marble Arch, Hyde Park Corner or V.C.S.

A code for the countryside

The Countryside Commission have prepared the Country Code as a guide to visitors, some of whom are perhaps unaccustomed to country ways. Please remember to observe the following standards of good manners when you go to enjoy the beauties and the pleasures of the garden that is Britain's countryside.

1 Guard against all risks of fire
Don't drop lighted matches or cigarette ends, particularly near crops, plantations, woods, heaths and hay ricks. A fire, once started, is difficult to put out.

2 Fasten all gates
Animals can do great damage to crops and to themselves if they stray. They may be injured by traffic or be the cause of accidents.

3 Keep dogs under proper control
Animals are easily frightened by strange dogs, so do not let them disturb cattle, hens or sheep; keep your dog on its lead when near other animals or walking along the road.

4 Keep to the paths across farm land
Avoid damaging crops in any way. Corn, grass and hay that have been trampled flat are difficult to harvest. Do not trespass.

5 Avoid damaging fences, hedges and walls
Where a man can go, an animal will follow, and damage to crops will result. Use gates and stiles where they are provided.

6 Do not leave litter

Take your litter home, including bottles and tins. All litter is not only unsightly but dangerous. Broken glass, opened tins and plastic bags can very easily harm livestock and damage farm machinery.

7 Safeguard water supplies

A stream, brook or well may be the only water supply for a farmer and his animals. Water is precious in the country. Do not pollute it in any way.

8 Protect wild life, plants amd trees

Never dig up plants and flowers, carve on trees, and please do not take birds' eggs. Wild flowers, birds and trees give more pleasure to more people if left alone.

9 Go carefully on country roads

Blind corners, hump-back bridges, slow-moving farm vehicles and herds of cattle are all hazards for the motorist, cyclist and walker. Careless car parking may block the entrance to fields or farmyards.

10 Respect the life of the countryside

Enjoy the countryside, but do not hinder the work of the countryman. Roads and paths run through the farmers' land, and animals, machinery and buildings are the raw materials from which he earns his living. You, the public, are on trust. Be considerate.

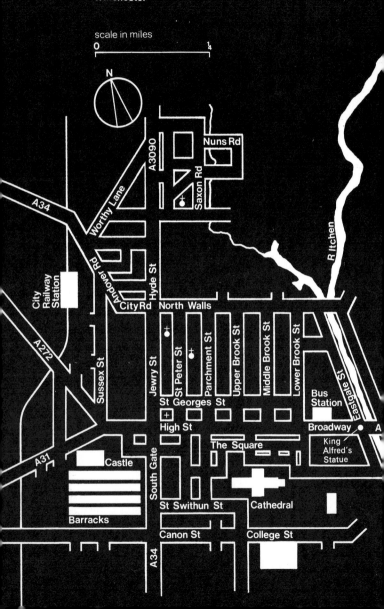

1

Part one River Itchen to River Wey

Winchester

Winchester, once the capital of England, lies within a fold of the Hampshire Downs and at an important crossing of the River Itchen. Easily accessible by road and rail from both London and the Midlands, Winchester is a city well worth exploring before we commence our modern pilgrimage.

Brief history

There was some settlement on the site of Winchester in the first century BC. During the Roman occupation the city, called Venta Belgarum, was the commercial and administrative centre for a tribal area covering a large part of what is now Hampshire, and at least five roads met here.

The Romans came about AD 44 and built great walls to enclose 138 acres of land, defended by ditches and the river. It is unusual in plan in that the main streets do not divide the city into four equal quarters. The crossing of these streets is close to the western wall, probably to avoid an exit upon the marshy lands beside the Itchen, which flowed against the eastern wall. The Romans constructed five great roads, radiating to Silchester, Marlborough, Old Sarum, Southampton and Porchester. What remains of the Roman town is now 8-12 feet down, and excavations have brought to light traces of the street-grid and of several buildings.

Winchester became the capital of Wessex under the Saxon Cerdic in c.519. A castle was built on the high ground in the south-west part of the fortified Roman area. There were then six gates into the city, but only two now remain—the West Gate at the top of High Street and the King's Gate to the south. Bishop Birinus came to Winchester in 635 and in 643 converted King Cenwealh to Christianity; a church was set up and this became the bishop's seat in 674, and was known as the Old Minster. The Bishop St Swithun (852-62) was buried outside the west door of this cathedral 'where the rains of heaven might fall upon him'.

After the Norman Conquest, William made Winchester his capital and the city became very prosperous. St Giles' Fair, granted by William Rufus to Bishop Walkelin for the building of the Cathedral, became the most famous in England, and was attended by merchants from all over Europe.

The city seems to have reached its zenith in the twelfth century. It was a battleground for seven weeks in 1141 and a great part of it was destroyed by fire. The city also suffered severely at the hands of Simon de Montfort the Younger in 1265, and was later devastated by the Black Death.

During the Civil War the City suffered much from its loyalty to Charles I, and its ancient castle, founded by WIlliam the Conqueror, was destroyed in 1645. Charles II intended to make Winchester a royal residence once again, and he began building a palace in 1683. It was unfinished at the time of his death in 1685 and became a barracks.

In the later half of the eighteenth century many of Winchester's historic buildings were removed. Most of the City Walls, together with the North, South and East Gates were pulled down, and many of the ancient features of the city disappeared.

King Alfred's statue, Winchester

39

The nineteenth century saw Winchester develop into a residential and educational centre and a place of pilgrimage for lovers of antiquity.

Winchester Cathedral

The Cathedral Church of the Holy Trinity, St Peter, St Paul, and St Swithun lies in a hollow and there are no dramatic distant views of it. It is only in the grassy Close that one realises its size, but the splendid interior belies its somewhat austere external appearance.

The Saxon cathedral was rebuilt under the Norman Bishop Walkelin in 1079, and was completed fourteen years later on 8 April 1093. Walkelin's masterpiece consisted of a nave, west front and central tower, flanked by two transepts, with aisles, crypt, choir and range of cloisters. The church thus rebuilt was the longest in western Europe, its nave being second only in length to St Peter's in Rome. The overall length of the great cathedral is 556 feet. The height of the nave vaulting is only 78 feet but its width at the transept's crossing is 231 feet. The height of the tower is 140 feet, and the building is largely of stone from the Isle of Wight.

On 15 July 1093 the relics of St Swithun were transferred from the old to the new building. Heaven's disapproval of the moving of the saint's body from its original modest resting place was shown by continuous rain for forty days, and the saint's name came to be associated in popular memory ever since with the fickleness of the English summer climate.

Bishop Godfrey de Lucy (1189-1204) began a reconstruction of the eastern part in 1202 by building a retro-choir and the Lady Chapel. St Swithun's shrine was moved from the south-east aisle of the nave to a more fitting place in the retro-choir, as it had already begun to attract great numbers of pilgrims. The shrine

Winchester Cathedral. The Nave, looking East

was destroyed and its treasures confiscated at the Dissolution in 1539, but a new shrine has been erected on its site.

A total remodelling of the nave was begun by Bishop William Edington (1346-66) by the west front, and continued by the transformation of the Norman nave into Early Perpendicular style by Bishop William of Wykeham (1366-1404). This tremendous undertaking resulted in one of the glories of Winchester, and completed the major construction works. Later additions were directed towards the elaboration of the interior—the Lady Chapel was remodelled by Bishop Courtenay (1486-92) and Bishop Langton (1493-1501) and the Chancel by Bishop Fox (1501-28). The beautiful chantry chapels are the various works of Bishops Edington, Wykeham, Beaufort, Waynflete, Langton and Fox.

Excavations made in 1957 and 1961 have located the Old and New Saxon Minsters and aim at their complete restoration. The Old Minster lies immediately north of the present nave, at a slight angle, so that the west end of the Minster is partly below the west end of the Cathedral. The New Minster was built in 903 and lies north of, and parallel to, the Old Minster, in places as little as three feet away. It was abandoned for a new site in 1110. In the late ninth century Alfred and his wife founded the Nun's Minster, but this has not been precisely located, although it is within the same monastic enclosure as the Old and New Minsters.

As the burial and coronation churches of many of the kings of Wessex and of England, these Minsters formed an ecclesiastical group without parallel in this country. The Bishopric is still one of the most important in the country, and carries with it the prelacy of the Order of the Garter.

Winchester Cathedral. The Choir, facing East.

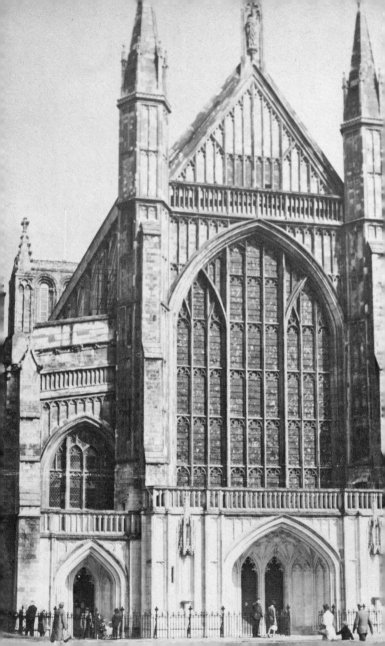

Other places of interest

The castle was built by William the Conqueror and was the birthplace of Henry III and Arthur, son of Henry VII. In it Henry VIII entertained the Emperor Charles V in 1522, who inspected the Round Table of King Arthur.

The Round Table is not older than the time of Henry III and was repainted by Henry VIII for Emperor Charles V's visit. It is 18 feet in diameter and painted in the Tudor colours of green and white. In the centre is a Tudor rose, surmounted by King Arthur, and it bears the names of twenty-four of his knights around the edge. It has been suggested that the Round Table may have been the chief tribunal or superior court of justice, and today it forms an impressive background at the Assize Courts in the Great Hall.

The Great Hall is all that remains of the castle after the Civil War in 1644-5. It was the seat of Parliament for centuries, and here was held the famous trial of Sir Walter Raleigh in 1603 for conspiracy against Charles I.

Winchester College was founded in 1382 by William of Wykeham (of 'Manners makyth man' fame), and is the oldest of the major public schools in England. The College was begun in 1387 and opened in 1394 to educate clergy in canon and civil law, and as an adjunct to Wykeham's New College in Oxford, founded 1379.

Wolvesey Castle, the palace of the medieval bishops of Winchester, was built by Bishop Henry de Blois (1129-71) in 1137. Here Queen Mary Tudor lodged before marrying Philip of Spain in the Cathedral in 1554, the last royal marriage in Winchester. The castle was levelled to the ground by the Parliamentarians in 1645. Only the chapel remains, and this adjoins the palace begun by Wren for Bishop Morley in 1683.

Winchester Cathedral

Henry de Blois's Hospital of St Cross dates from about 1133. It is the oldest institution of its kind in the country and was founded for 'thirteen poor impotent men so reduced in strength as rarely or never to be able to raise themselves without the assistance of another'. In the porter's hatchway under the tower is provided a 'wayfarers dole', of bread and beer to all comers—so long as the daily ration lasts. The hospital lies one mile south of the city centre and may be approached by the west bank of the River Itchen. It is unfortunately on the wrong side of the city to be visited by the modern pilgrim travelling up the valley towards Alresford.

The City Mill dates from 1743-7 and is now owned by the National Trust and open to the public. It has been converted into a youth hostel, and hostellers have the unusual experience of washing in the mill race.

There are many other ancient buildings in Winchester to see, but within the centre of the city some old street frontages have disappeared and with them a number of interesting buildings. Yet much of the essential charm of Winchester remains and an observant visitor must carry away with him the memory and atmosphere of a great cathedral and its small-scale streets.

We begin our journey from the great West Door of
Winchester Cathedral and bear half-right along the
paved path between the avenue of trees to a road at
The Square, passing the City Museum on our right
just outside the cathedral precincts. Cross over the
road into the cul-de-sac street where stands St Lawrence's, a church built upon the site of William the
Conqueror's Chapel Royal.

Pass under the Pentice archway to emerge at the
High Street by the beautiful High Cross, perhaps the
finest Perpendicular cross in England. The cross was
erected about 1450 in the reign of Henry VI and
restored in 1865. High Street is a picturesque and
bustling thoroughfare on which all other streets
converge at right-angles, and as in Roman times is still
the spine of the town, though now partly pedestrian-
ised and bypassed by city centre traffic.

Turn left along High Street and after 20 yards or
so just before Lloyds Bank with its projecting door
turn right along narrow St Peter's Street to the
crossing of St George's Street. On the left-hand side is
the site of the church of St Peter, where the curfew
bell tolled for many centuries. It is one of the sites of
the many vanished parish churches of medieval
Winchester.

Continue ahead along St Peter's Street. On the

right hand is the Royal Hotel, once a Benedictine
convent, and a little way further on is Avebury
House, built 1690, with a very elegant Doric doorcase
with Tuscan columns and a fluted frieze. As we
follow the street we also pass a Methodist church and
a Catholic church, soon to come to the junction with
North Street.

Turn left in North Street to the traffic lights at the
A34 cross-roads. At this point stood the North Gate,
but it was demolished in 1756 and only a plaque
remains to mark its site. Here the pilgrims left the
walled city and took the old road now followed by
Hyde Street.

If you can, continue past the red-brick Hyde
Brewery, built 1821, for a few hundred yards to King
Alfred Place. Turn right into this little street to the
church of St Bartholomew, built 1185 for the tenants
and servants of the Abbots of the Abbey of St Peter
and St Grimbald. Hyde Abbey was a famous Benedictine monastery founded by Alfred and his son
Edward, and the establishment was moved here in the
reign of Henry I. The present remains of the abbey,
which was destroyed in the Reformation of 1538, are
the gateway to the Abbot's Lodgings, the mill stream
and its bridges, and some fragments in St Bartholomew's church. King Alfred was buried in the abbey,
but his bones were not disinterred as were others in
the Reformation. His leaden coffin was dug up un-
opened in the building of the prison (now vanished)
and sold in 1788 for £2.

Follow a path for a few yards with the church on
your right, soon to reach Saxon Road. When this
bends sharp left turn slightly right and cross over a
stream into Nuns Road, then immediately turn left,
opposite a telephone call-box, along a footpath,
through a turnstile and so into open fields.

High Cross, Winchester High Street

Winchester to Alresford 9 miles

This stream now on our left is one of several drainage
channels in the Itchen valley, and we keep beside it
for nearly two miles, the only stretch of proper footpath between Winchester and Farnham.

After a few hundred yards cross a stile ahead and
keep straight on again along a clear track to a smallholding ahead opposite a thatched cottage. Here turn
left over the stream by a bridge and and immediately
right again along a path, with weeping willows lining
the bank of the stream on your right. After a while
the path crosses the stream again beside a water pipe,
then bears slightly right to a stile beside the main
stream of the River Itchen.

Modern roadworks, being the continuation of the
Winchester Bypass, have caused the diversion of
the original footpath, but at this stile beside the river
you can see the line of the old path striking half-left
across the field. Climb the stile and turn sharp left
with the new road on your right. Continue for a few
hundred yards, then turn right under the road by a
new pedestrian subway. Pass under the arch ahead
and then immediately turn left along a narrow
path at the foot of the embankment and past a
factory making tubular sheathed heating elements,
where the path is called Nun's Walk. Where the driveway to this factory turns left continue straight on,
with a line of trees on your right, coming soon into
the graveyard on the south side of Kings Worthy
Church.

This path from Winchester is probably the original
track, variously known as the Monk's or the Nun's
Walk, but there is an alternative along the line of the
modern road A33 passing Headbourne Worthy. This
main road is above the level of marshy land, avoids
the crossing of any stream, and indicates the contin-
uity of the Worthy villages as a string of similar sites
of similar antiquity.

Winchester Cathedral

The track we have just followed, however, is
shorter and follows the edge of the chalk and just
avoids the marshy alluvial soil of the valley. The
Bourne stream from Headbourne Worthy has been
diverted, embanked along the Monk's Walk, presumably for the purpose of giving power to the mill
at Hyde Abbey and supplying that community with
water. The Monastery presumably would have had its
gates upon the oldest highway of its time: the Roman
road also took the same line, straight from the North
Gate of Winchester to Kings Worthy Church.

The Church of St Mary, Kings Worthy, is mostly
thirteenth century, though it was over-restored in
1864. The polygonal vestry is perhaps the only feature
one may remember in this church. After Kings Worthy
the modern roads B3047 and A31 correspond with
the ancient track for the next 16 miles to Alton,
although there is a footpath through to Itchen Abbas
which meanders on a lower level by the river.

Follow the B3047 for nearly 5 miles past the
hamlets of Abbots Worthy, Martyr Worthy and
Itchen Abbas to Itchen Stoke. The churches of St
Swithun, Martyr Worthy, and St John Baptist, Itchen
Abbas, lie just south of this road.

The Church of St John Baptist, Itchen Abbas, is a
Neo-Norman style building built in 1867 on a cruciform plan. In the churchyard is an ancient yew tree
and under its branches is the grave of one John
Hughes, aged 26, hanged at Westminster on 19 March
1823, for horse stealing. It is said that he was the last
man to be hanged in England for that offence.

Two miles east of Itchen Abbas lies Itchen Stoke
where the Pilgrims' Way crossed the river. The valley
of the Itchen here makes a sharp bend northwards
round a low but rather difficult hill and leads on to
the Alresfords, and the modern London-Winchester
road A31 follows this line. The old road crossed the
river, crested Tichborne Down and joined the London

The crossing of the River Alre at Itchen Stoke

road by the church at Bishops Sutton, one mile east of New Alresford.

'Stoke', as is usual in places by rivers, means an artificial causeway or crossing of the water, and here the river is shallow, the bottom firm, and the banks not too widely separated. Just above Itchen Stoke is the confluence of the Itchen, Alre and other streams, and as such a confluence is invariably marshy this could not have been avoided save by a long bend to the north, where no trace of a track exists. On the south of Itchen Stoke there is a steep dry bank on which to continue one's journey. An old church once stood by the river in such a position that the road to the ford passed just by its southern porch, but this interesting place disappeared in 1831.

It is true that an ancient trackway leaves Old Alresford to the north-east, but this does not point direct to Farnham, the known junction of the short cut. Old Alresford is too far to the west and north of

the track we have been following to be visited save by an abrupt and inexplicable bend. New Alresford is nearer to this track, though not on it, but it was not in existence till the twelfth century, whereas a bishop's palace had stood for some centuries at Sutton close by, hence Bishops Sutton.

As has been and will be seen, a high but narrow watershed has to be crossed between Winchester and Farnham. To approach this watershed by the easiest route, avoiding marshy ground, one would cross the ford at Itchen Stoke and go straight across the hill to Bishops Sutton and then follow in a direct line to one's object. The hill south of Alresford afforded a view ahead, and a direct advance upon the ridge of the watershed could be planned eastwards under the advancing night.

Immediately opposite the Church of St Mary, Itchen Stoke, 1866, take the lane down to the river, signposted 'Footpath to Ovington', to a foot-bridge. Cross this and follow a beautiful footpath between the streams of the crystal clear river to another footbridge which leads to the 'Bush' at Ovington. Follow the road between streams and uphill to cross the dual carriageway of A31. Take the road immediately opposite, and where this bends right take the lane on the left. Cross a minor road, then the River Itchen by a footbridge over a deep ford, to reach the 'Cricketers Arms' at road B3046. New Alresford lies ¾ mile to the left, down the hill, and we will return to this point when we have visited this little town.

New Alresford

Alresford (pronounced Allsford) was once a prosperous country town with a flourishing trade, though now it is a large village depending on Winchester and Alton.

Church of St John Baptist, New Alresford

57

The town was founded and laid out by Bishop
Godfrey de Lucy (1189-1204) in 1200 when he
built a great dam across the River Itchen to form a
reservoir of 200 acres to make the river navigable
down to Southampton at all seasons. The reservoir
has since shrunk, but it is still beautiful and large
enough to attract a great many water birds.

The main street, Broad Street, runs north from the
Winchester road and is the best village street in
Hampshire. The broad street is lined with two rows of
lime trees and flanked by rendered houses, making it
agreeable without exception. The great house by the
church was built by one of our greatest naval heroes,
Admiral Lord Rodney (1719-92), and he is credited
with the building of most of the pubs in the village.
There are a great many spaced out on opposite sides
of the straight road, spaced, so it has been said, in
order that the Admiral might 'tack' from one to the
other and home again. He is buried in Old Alresford
church.

The Church of St John Baptist, New Alresford, lies
just to the south of the main junction of the
streets. The flint church dates mostly from 1898,

Above: Napoleonic tombstones in New Alresford graveyard
Right: Jane Austen's house, Chawton

though the west tower is early fourteenth century and has a seventeenth century brick top. French names on five tombstones in the churchyard recall that French prisoners were quartered here in the Napoleonic wars.

Alresford to Alton 10 miles

From the 'Cricketers Arms' at road B3046 and with Alresford Golf Course on your right continue over Tichbourne Down and steeply down White Hill Lane to Bishops Sutton, a place so called because here was once a residence of the Bishops of Winchester.

The Norman Church of St Nicholas is built of flints, with a brick porch and weatherboarded bell-turret. There are two noteworthy Norman doorways, both with weird half-human birds' heads, and some Norman windows in the north and south walls of the wide nave.

The modern highway A31 corresponds to the old road as far as the 'Chequers Inn' at Ropley, following the lowest part of the valley. But here the valley

curves north, and it might be presumed that the
original way, making more directly for the saddle of
the watershed, would gradually climb the southern
hillside. By doing so it would have the dual advant-
ages of taking a shorter cut and conquering at one
stretch, and rapidly, the rise of 350 feet from the inn
to the summit.

However, the old road does not follow the valley
but takes a straight line upwards direct to the
summit, and traces of the old track can be seen in its
early stages. The place-name 'Street' is a guide, as it is
a word invariably found in connection with an
ancient roadway—to the south of this line is Gilbert
Street and north of it is North Street. (Other examples are West Street and Broad Street near Lenham,
Dunn Street near Eastwell, and the old name for
Albury—Weston Street.)

Just after the Bighton-Ropley cross-road at Ropley
Dean, a few hundred yards before the 'Chequers
Inn', in a field on the right is an embankment,
perfectly straight, turning slightly away from the
main road and pointing directly towards the saddle. It
may continue through the garden of 'Chequers Inn',
but in a few fields beyond it has entirely disappeared
and cannot be followed. It would have crossed the
Gilbert Street-North Street road just south of Manor
Farm and entered Brislands Lane, which takes the hill
steeply and continues straight to the saddle.

Brislands Lane runs wide and straight for two miles
or so, and after a cross-road continues as Blackberry
Lane, passing through an extraordinary collection of
bungalows and wooden cottages which have mush-
roomed upon either side. At the summit bend left to
the thirteenth milestone on the London road, A31,
which has been climbing the valley below through
Four Marks. The line of the old road continues ahead
through a wood but is lost among the houses built
along Farringdon Lane. Here one finally leaves the

valley of the Itchen to join that of the Wey.

At the point where the old road leaves the wood it is joined by the London road which continues as far as Alton and to just beyond Farnham, a distance of 14 miles. For 2 miles the road follows the bottom of the valley, falling in that distance some 300 feet. It descends by the easiest gradient, for had it taken to the hillside it would have fallen at last upon Alton by way of a steep spur.

The valley road leads straight ahead, but after the roundabout it turns right to join the Meon valley road, A32, at Chawton, where Jane Austen lived for the last seven years of her life.

Jane Austen's house stands at the corner of the Winchester and Alton roads, A31 and A32, and is open daily to the public. The modest, square, two-storeyed red-brick house was her home from 1809 to 1817. Here she revised 'Sense and Sensibility' and 'Pride and Prejudice' and wrote 'Mansfield Park', 'Emma' and 'Persuasion'. These later novels aroused great enthusiasm and drew forth high praise from such men as Lord Macauley and Sir Walter Scott.

The old road did not pass through Chawton but would have continued to enter Alton at its south-west end, at the same point by which an ancient road from Old Alresford via Medstead entered the town.

However, the ground has lost all its original character because the railway embankments have obliterated everything. Immediately after the roundabout at the end of the Alton Bypass A31 take the road on the left. Pass under the railway arch and at the end of the road turn right.

On the left after ½ mile is the Lord Mayor Treolar Hospital, a vast institution for cripples founded in 1908 by Sir William Purdie Treolar (1843-1923), Lord Mayor of London in 1906-7. Pass under another railway arch, cross road B3006 and along Butts Road beside a green to enter the High Street at Alton.

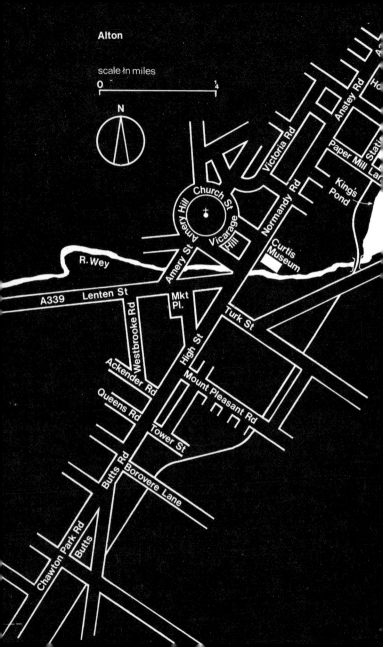

Alton stands at the head of the Wey valley and is an ancient borough. In the eighteenth century there was a considerable industry in silks and woollen cloths, but these have now disappeared and brewing is the main business today. There are several sixteenth- and seventeenth-century houses camouflaged by modern fronts and some genuine ones, and picturesque old inns in the main street.

Winchester Road and All Saints Church, 1873, leads us into the High Street, where there is a Wesleyan Chapel of 1846 in the Italianate style, with arched windows. After a stretch Market Street leads off to the left to the small Market Place. Leading off this is Amery Street which hides a small house where Edmund Spenser, the great Elizabethan poet, lived in 1590.

Market Street continues as Lenten Street and at No. 25 was born on 11 January 1746 the world-famous botanist William Curtis. Curtis founded the 'Botanical Magazine', and with his family, all of whom were interested in natural history, founded the Curtis Museum in 1855. This is housed in a building at the top of High Street and should be visited by everyone who has the chance. It contains a valuable collection of bygone agricultural implements, china and Roman pottery, and old views of the town.

Opposite the Curtis Museum runs Church Street,

Pages 64-65: Alton High Street

leading to the interesting parish Church of St
Lawrence. It is one of the very rare churches which
have two naves and two chancels. St Lawrence's is a
Perpendicular town church built round an Early
Norman crossing tower. This now stands in the south
aisle, for in the fifteenth century a new nave and
chancel were built north of the previous church. At
the same time the former nave was rebuilt and alter-
ations made to the chancel. The exterior of the
church is fifteenth century throughout, except for a
Victorian broach spire.

In the Civil War the town was held by 80 Royalists
under Colonel Richard Boles, but they had to retreat
to the church under the heavy fire of the Round-
heads. The great south door and walls show the scars
of the fight, for deeply embedded in the timbers are
still some of the actual bullets. A brass tablet on one
of the pillars in the nave, a replica of the original in
Winchester Cathedral, tells the story of Boles, who
died serving the Royalists on 13 December 1641.

Return to the High Street and continue eastwards
along Normandy Street, passing the stuccoed Con-
gregational Chapel, 1835, then along Anstey Road
leading out of town, past the Infirmary, 1793, with
its mansard roof, and the Grammar School which was
founded in 1638.

The pilgrims usually travelled by the main track
through the valley, as this was the easiest and quickest
way of reaching Farnham, and it is now the main
road. This stretch has several pecularities:
1 It follows the River Wey for miles, not as it
followed the River Itchen, on a dry ledge above the
stream, but right along the low land of the waterside.
It is within easy reach of the water for men and
animals, but avoids the low levels, thick cover and
danger of floods. The nearness of the track to a river
is not to be found in any other part of its course—be
it Itchen, Mole, Darent, Medway or Stour.

Holybourne church

2 In every other stretch of its length the old road passes along the edge of villages and farmed land, but here it forms the main streets of Alton, Bentley and Farnham.

3 There is the correspondence between the old road and the modern road for the whole of this considerable distance, a character which is unique. It so remained identical up to and beyond its point of junction with the older 'Harrow Way' at Farnham.

An explanation for this coincidence is that the hills which everywhere else afford so even a platform for the prehistoric road are here of a contour which forbids their use. Any road down this valley must have run upon this lowest line. There are deep coombes at Holybourne Down, two at Froyle, one at Bentley and another before Farnham. Any path attempting these hillsides would either have doubled its length by avoiding the hollows, or would have been a succession of steep ascents and descents had it remained direct. All the dry slopes which bound the valley to the north are a succession of steep and isolated projections, and the road is compelled to take to the valley floor.

As far as Froyle, 3 miles from Alton, the road never leaves the river by more than ¼ mile, but the valley here is dry, a narrow strip of gravel. For 2 miles after Froyle there is clay, but the road follows greensand. At the entry to Bentley village the clay is unavoidable, but after a mile of it the road takes advantage of a patch of gravel on the 300-foot contour as far as the 'Bull Inn', avoiding the marshy levels. Then to within 2 miles of Farnham the road has to negotiate a good deal of clay, but it picks out a long irregular and narrow patch of gravel, and at the end of this, just east of the county boundary, it finds the narrow belt of sand again, which it keeps to all the way to Farnham on the low level without difficulty.

Though the valley is full of clay, the road avoids it

with remarkable success, and the whole is an example
of how a primitive track will avoid bad soil. The old
road keeps throughout this passage to the sunny
northern bank of the river, so that while it is compelled to keep to the bottom of the valley, it attempts at
least to get the driest part of it.

Holybourne is a straggling continuation of Alton
on the Farnham road, and we pass south of Froyle
and Bentley to leave Hampshire just 2 miles west of
Farnham. At the roundabout at the junction of roads
A31 and A325 bear left along A325 to enter Farnham at West Street.

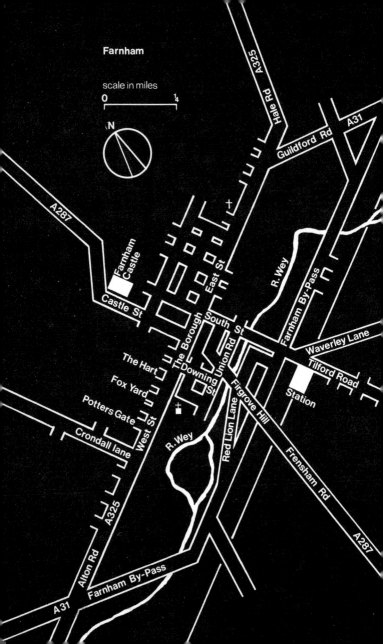

Farnham lies in a dip carved out by the River Wey,
which flows south of the ridge to break through at
Guildford on its way to the Thames. Being at the
mouth of this valley, Farnham was a common meeting-
place of travellers coming from all directions. It is at
the junction of the old road and its still older pre-
decessor from Salisbury Plain, and was always a place
of importance—the meeting-place of roads from
Salisbury Plain, the Channel, from London and the
Straits of Dover.

Farnham was the greatest market town in England
for wheat and had thriving hop fields, though it is
now mainly a stockbroker suburb. It has many
attractive Georgian buildings and is generally
regarded as one of the best Georgian towns in
England: two superb set-pieces are grouped in West
Street and Castle Street, but there is a depressing
amount of Neo-Georgian throughout the rest of the
town.

We will begin our exploration of the town as we
enter at the west end along the long main street,
here called West Street. Immediately we come upon
the two show houses of Farnham, side by side on the
south side of the street—No. 39, Sandford House,
built 1757, and No. 38, Wilmer House, built 1718.
Both show the same sort of Baroque style, but the

older Wilmer House has one of the finest cut-brick facades in the country. The house is now the town's museum and includes personalia of William Cobbett, of 'Rural Rides' fame.

Beyond, continuing towards the centre, is Vernon House, originally sixteenth century but re-done in 1727. It is now the public library. Charles I stayed for a night here with Harry Vernon on 20 December 1648, on his way from Hurst Castle to London as a prisoner to his trial, and it was here that he met the Roundhead general Thomas Harris who was soon to sign his death warrant.

Opposite, on the north side, Nos. 88 to 94 are the best formal group in Farnham, all plain houses of 1760-80 except No. 94 which is a clever piece of twentieth-century building. This group shows eighteenth-century town housing at its very best; there is nothing so good as this further east. 'The Surrey and Hants' News office is a converted eighteenth-century house and the 'Lion and Lamb', with close timbers and brick infilling, dates from 1537.

At the end of West Street Downing Street runs off to the south to the Church of St Andrew, one of the largest in Surrey. The church has grown up from a Norman cross-shaped building, with a very long narrow nave and chancel and with wide aisles. It dates mostly from the early fifteenth century, but was so violently restored in 1855 that little but the medieval proportions remain. The best part is the impressive west tower with polygonal buttresses, left unfinished at the Reformation but completed with a nineteenth-century top which looks like a fortress. About the church are many beautiful and interesting tributes to Farnham people—windows, stone inscriptions, brasses and monuments; old, quaint and fascinating.

Return up Downing Street to the West Street junction and turn right into the Borough, the narrow centre section of the main road. The National Westminster

Nos 38 and 39 West Street, Farnham

Bank has an Italianate front of 1860 and lies slap on
the axis of Castle Street, the tallest building on this
frontage and closing the view from the castle.

Castle Street, the former market place, runs north
from the centre of Downing Street and sweeps up to
the south side of the castle, which is seen above the
trees, and then side-steps just at the last moment.
Houses of 1750-1850 combine to make an impressive
example of townscape, the group of Nos. 12 to 42 on
the west side being particularly fine.

Farnham Castle

A flight of steps at the top of Castle Street leads to
the castle, which stands on the site where King
Alfred's son, Edward, defeated the Danes in 893. The
castle stands proudly on its hill, and those who climb
to the top are rewarded with wide views of Farnham
and the sweeping Downs.

The earliest structure was probably an earthen
motte thrown up by Bishop Walkelin, and the castle
remained the residence of the bishops of Winchester
until 1927. Parts of it are still used as the residence of
their successors, the bishops of Guildford, and others
are under the guardianship of the Department of the
Environment. The keep is open to the public, but
the rest is privately occupied. The castle is one of the
best examples of a twelfth-century domestic castle
in the country.

The great shell keep was built round the motte by
Bishop Henry de Blois (1129-71) and he also built the
triangular bailey, in which is the bishop's residence.
The group of domestic buildings adjoining this central
core date from the same period, but they have been
much transformed as the castle grew in significance
down the centuries.

To this episcopal palace came the greatest church-
men in the land. Here lived William of Wykeham,

Castle Street, Farnham

builder of Winchester; William of Waynflete, Lord
Chancellor and founder of Magdalen College; Cardinal
Beaufort, who saw Joan of Arc burned in the market
place of Rouen; and Cardinal Wolsey with his master
Henry VIII. They were followed by Mary I, who was
entertained here by Bishop Gardiner on her way to
marry Philip of Spain at Winchester in 1554; here
Elizabeth I delivered her famous warning to the Duke
of Norfolk (then planning to marry Mary, Queen of
Scots) to beware on what pillow he laid his head.
There are also recorded visits to the castle by James I,
George III, and by Queen Victoria.

   South of the River Wey is the 'Jolly Farmers' in
Bridge Square where William Cobbett was born in
1762. A farmer's boy and soldier, he became a public-
ist and reformer, and was goaled in 1810 for his
political opinions. When he died in 1835 he left in his
writings a rich heritage of fine thoughts finely
expressed. Of these his 'Rural Rides', collected from
his 'Political Register', are the most famous. They
describe the English countryside and the sufferings of
the exploited agricultural poor, the problems of home
and farm, of estate and kingdom, and his work is a
memorial to the death of old rural England.

Farnham to Seale 4 miles

Farnham was the common meeting-place of travellers
coming from all directions and it was from here that
all the western tracks proceeded to the Straits of
Dover, or rather Canterbury, the rallying-point of the
several Kentish ports.

   There were three ways to Guildford. Those in a
hurry sped along the chalk ridge of the Hog's Back,
but the great majority followed the lower track,
below the ridge, on a straight line through Seale and
Puttenham to St Catherine's Ferry on the River Wey.
Many would follow this second route as far as Puttenham and then make the diversion to Compton, to

Seale church

rejoin the main route at St Catherine's.

From the centre of Farnham continue along East Street for nearly a mile, passing a good many old houses but nothing of real interest. Bear right along Guildford Road and continue ahead at the modern intersection of A31 with the Farnham Bypass. The road rises, and at the junction bear right, crossing over the railway.

At this point just outside the town the road begins to rise; an indication that it is about to take to the flank of the hills, a position which it holds uninterruptedly (save for four short gaps occasioned by four river valleys) until just before Canterbury.

The rise continues gradually until the 'Jolly Farmer' at Runfold and the fork at Whiteways. Here the main road bends sharply left to take in the ridge of the Hog's Back, while the old road continues ahead, 200 feet below, on the side of the hill to Seale. As you enter the village bear right, and after a few hundred yards you reach the church.

Seale church stands on a little mound and the

track passed south of it, not right against its porch,
but as near as it can. The church was built at the
expense of Waverley in the period of enthusiasm that
followed the first pilgrimages, just after 1200. The
timber porch is six hundred years old and is perhaps
the most impressive thing in the church, though there
are interesting and tragic memorials, and one of the
six bells in the tower was made three hundred years
ago.

Seale to Puttenham 2 miles

Just to the south of the church, by the war memorial,
the road bends left along the flank of a hill, passing
East End Farm, a group of buildings round a fine
sixteenth-century timbered house with striking
chimneys. In another mile we come to Shoelands, a
Tudor House with parts dating from 1616. Its name
has been connected with 'schooling', or almsgiving.

Puttenham village consists of one long street in a
pretty situation just south of the Hog's Back, fortunately not yet the nine-storey-high village with poultry
farm and vitamin factory of a 'Brave New World'. It
lies on the exact dividing line between chalk and
sandstone, so the cottages use both, with a lot of
brickwork also. Just before the church is reached is
Greys Home Farm with a good set of weatherboarded
barns, including a range of four oasthouses, a rarity in
the county, now converted into dwellings.

Just before entering the centre of the village from
the west the Pilgrims' Way turns a sharp corner, so
much against its nature that there must be an explanation for it. The present road goes round to the north
of the church, outside a high wall, which therefore
forbids any passage. It turns sharp round a corner and
proceeds due south along road B3000 to the 'Jolly
Farmer' inn. The old road has been lost in the village
and it is probable that it passed south of the church

The Pilgrims' Way on Puttenham Heath passing beneath the

A3 Guildford Road

direct to the 'Jolly Farmer'. The road through the
village, the south porch of the church and the front
of the inn are all in the same alignment, and short of
any physical obstacle, there is no reason but private
property, and property long established and defined,
to give rise to such an unnatural and sudden right-
angled turn in the road.

The medieval details of the Church of St John
Baptist merge into a clumsy restoration of 1861, but
the inside still keeps plastered walls and a pleasant
village appearance. The fifteenth-century tower
patched with red brick lost its spire in a fire 200 years
ago, and we enter the church through the unusually
decorated south porch dating from 1170. The oddest
thing about the nave arcade columns is that their
bases rise from bay to bay as if the floor had originally been kept at an incline. The four-bay north
arcade has windows of 1160 and there are other
renewed twelfth-century features. The chancel is very
attractive with its modern oak panelling and carvings,
and has mainly Perpendicular windows. There is a
20-inch high brass on the chancel floor of Edward
Cranford, rector of the church c.1430, and a charge is
made to take a rubbing.

To the south of the church stands Puttenham
Priory, a handsome provincial Palladian house of
1762. The main front looks west, and is faced with
golden stucco in a very good imitation of stone. The
picturesque Tudor building among trees just east of
the church is the Rectory.

From the road junction at the top of the street
beside the church bear right to the 'Jolly Farmer'. We
have now come 34 miles from Winchester, and except
for the first 2 miles the route has followed principally
a busy highway and other metalled roads. At this
point, however, now we have gained the chalk ridge,
we leave the main roads behind and continue our
journey along pleasant tracks and footpaths.

Puttenham to Compton 2 miles

From the 'Jolly Farmer' the road B3000 continues
south to the village of Compton before turning
eastwards towards the Wey, and pious pilgrims probably travelled this route to visit Compton church.
We must also visit Compton, but we will first follow
the main track over Puttenham Heath before making
the short diversion to the village.

Directly opposite the 'Jolly Farmer' take the left-
hand rough cart track passing 'Pilgrims Way Cottage'
on your right beside the golf club house. The track
runs clearly at the left edge of the heath beside a
hedge and you keep straight on along it, keeping the
golf course on your right. When the gravelly track
bears left keep right along a sandy track, and at the
next fork keep left, i.e. straight ahead. Pass beyond a
modern bungalow and a few cottages and when the
golf course ends on the right pass between thick
saplings to a broad crossing track.

This broad dirt track comes in from the left from
Monkshatch and continues south to the A3 at the
junction with B3000. The old road disappears at this
crossing, but 350 yards ahead a slightly sunken way
reappears. Cross the Monkshatch track to a path
opposite running along the foot of a wooded slope
known as Hurt Hill and after 750 yards pass under
the main road A3 by an archway. Here we join the
track from the farm we have just passed and continue
to a road, passing on the left hand the driveway up to
'Limnerslease'.

'Limnerslease' was the home of the great artist of
Compton and the late Victorian era, G. F. Watts, OM
RA (1817-1904). From 'Limnerslease' the Watts
Gallery is just up the road to the left. It stands behind
the building which formerly housed the Potters' Art
Guild, founded by Mrs G. F. Watts in 1903, and
contains hundreds of his great paintings, sculptures

and sketches. It is open to the public every afternoon
and Wednesday and Saturday mornings, but is closed
on Thursdays.

We must make the short detour to see the church
at nearby Compton, for it is believed to have been
visited by many pilgrims on their way eastwards. It
has a unique upper sanctuary which is thought to
have contained important relics.

Halfway along the road to Compton we come to a
cemetery with the Watts Mortuary Chapel, one of the
most curious and one of the least-known ecclesiastical
edifices in the country. Mrs Watts designed this
terracotta burial chapel in 1896 for her husband, and
it was built in local materials by local men and
plastered by trained villagers who worked in the
pottery which she had founded.

Inside and out it is covered with scores of mystic
symbols. The outside is a mixture of Italian Romanesque motifs and heavy Victorian symbolism. A great
frieze runs round the outside walls and shows on the
east face Hope, next Truth, then Love and finally
Light. Angel faces look down inside the triple arch of
the doorway, which has a wrought-iron cross copied
from a gravestone at Iona.

The remarkable interior was designed in 1901 and
is pure Art Nouveau—a very startling and effective
room with angels and cherubs and heavy colours of
gold, red and green. The silver roots of the Tree of
Life decorate the walls below and in the roof is the
Circle of Eternity. On the walls are four great groups of
angels, all carrying three pairs of symbols; on entering
the doorway these are, clockwise: Day and Night,
Flow and Ebb, Growth and Decay; next Life and
Death, Good and Evil, Labour and Rest; then Joy and
Sorrow, Spirit and Flesh, Real and Ideal; and finally
Freedom and Limit, Union and Conflict, Stability
and Change. The walls are also covered with mystical
work in ruby plaster and gilded: there are over 100

The Watts Mortuary Chapel, Compton

medallions and winged cherubs. There is a picture by
Watts painted to express the idea of the All-
Pervading, with suns and rolling systems in the lap of
a great enfolding figure encompassed by the hands of
Love.

One-quarter of a mile further down the road we
come to the Church of St Nicholas, Compton, on the
north side of the village. It is mainly a Norman
church with great round pillars and timber roof, but
it has a Saxon tower, impressively plain, unbutt-
ressed, and with simple rectangular openings.

The fame of Compton church is in its remarkable
chancel, quite unlike any other church in England. It
is one of the smallest but has a two-storey sanctuary,
and no one has yet been able to give a reason for it.

The first Norman chancel arch was built about
1080 and then 100 years later when the style was
changing into English the remarkable upper storey
was added. Two arches, one set back inside the other,
rest on round columns bedded in circular bases on
square plinths, and carry the upper sanctuary; the
columns are entirely of chalk, with beautifully carved
capitals which lead the eye up to the inside of the
arches, where the coating of the Norman plaster is cut
into a unique decoration.

The two-storey sanctuary is enclosed by a little
chancel screen with nine simple arches cut out of one
piece of oak or chestnut, one of the earliest and sole
surviving examples of Norman church woodwork in
the country. The little stone chamber which leads up
the steps to the upper storey was once the home of a
hermit.

When the interest of the chancel and its sancturies
are exhausted there are many other splendid works to
investigate in the church. Compton, with its Church
of St Nicholas and Watts Chapel and Gallery, must be
one of the most interesting places we visit along the
line of the Pilgrims' Way.

Interior of the Watts Mortuary Chapel, Compton

Compton to Guildford 3 miles

The Pilgrims' Way from Compton continues as a
public bridleway passing immediately south of the
Watts Gallery. It is a pretty, sunken, tree-lined path
that lives up to its name of Sandy Lane, and this is
followed for 2 miles out to a road at a sharp corner,
known as Littleton Cross. The Way follows the road
which ascends steeply, though in a cutting as before,
then drops steeply down to the A3100 Guildford
road, to the 'Ship' inn. Turn right along the road,
slightly uphill, and after 20 yards turn squarely left
down Ferry Lane.

St Catherine's Chapel stands on a curious platform
on the crest of the hill just to the south of Ferry
Lane and beside the main road. It is believed that there
was a chapel here seven hundred years ago, but the
ruins of the walls we see are early fourteenth century. Nobly have they stood the storms of time, but
the feeble iron railings hardly prevent vandals from
advancing its destruction.

Although it appears obvious from the map, the
exact spot at which the River Wey is crossed is not
easily determined, but the Pilgrims' Way appears on
the other side, half a mile away, by the north-west
corner of Chantries Wood.

There is a precipitous face towards the river and
the summit of St Catherine's Hill is isolated and
commands views up and down the valley. It would
have been a site sacred to a primitive tribe, and such
men would have chosen a ford over the river rather
than a ferry, and the ford exists. It has given its name
'the shallow ford' to the village of Shalford, which
grew up near it, with the church standing close by. So
it would appear that the Pilgrims' Way would pass
over the crest of St Catherine's, come down to the
south and cross to Shalford; but from Shalford to
Chantries Wood no track is apparent, and no passage

The Pilgrims' Way, Sandy Lane, Compton

Chantries Wood

could be made to Shalford except by a detour much
sharper than the old road executes in any other part
of its course.

However, a sunken way of great antiquity leads
directly from St Catherine's Hill down to the river. It
follows the only practicable descent of the bank, and
at its foot is a ferry, amd beyond a path crosses a
field, crosses the main road A281 and leads immediately and without any diversion to the corner of
Chantries Wood. Perhaps the passage at Shalford was
used first, and soon replaced by the ferry a little way
down stream.

Ferry Lane crosses the railway in a deep cutting
and then drops steeply down to the River Wey. After
having crossed the railway, notice Pilgrim Cottage on
the left, with a mosaic of St Christopher, the Patron
Saint of Travellers, on the chimney stack.

St Catherine's Ferry operates during the summer
season, at weekends and occasionally at other times.
The Countryside Commission proposes that a footbridge be built over the River Wey at this point on
the North Downs Way. Those who cannot or do not
wish to cross the river should, on reaching the ferry,
turn left and follow the river downstream on a footpath. After ¾ mile we enter Guildford by St Nicholas'
Church at the bottom of the High Street.

Pages 96-97: St Catherine's Chapel, Shalford

5

Part two River Wey to River Mole

Guildford to Dorking 12 miles

Guildford

Guildford is an interesting and ancient town with an old castle and a modern cathedral. The steep, cobbled High Street was declared by Dickens to be the most beautiful in the kingdom, but then he didn't see plate glass shopfronts and traffic congestion spoiling its character. In and around this street cluster all Guildford's ancient places, the centre-piece of attraction being the quaint sixteenth-century Guildhall and its magnificent overhanging seventeenth-century clock. The case is original and was made in 1683, but modern works have replaced the original works made in 1560. Notice the nice ironwork and also the buttresses upholding the little balcony, carved like ships' figureheads.

There are several places to see and visit in Guildford—the Tudor Royal Free Grammar School founded by Edward VI in 1553; the Jacobean gatehouse of the Abbot's Hospital, founded as an almshouse in 1619 by George Abbot, Archbishop of Canterbury; the castle keep and the Yvonne Arnaud Theatre, 1965, beside the river. The Rev C. L. Dodgson, better known as Lewis Carroll, died in the house called 'The Chestnuts' near the castle in 1898 and is buried in Guildford cemetery.

One must not fail also to visit the massive new

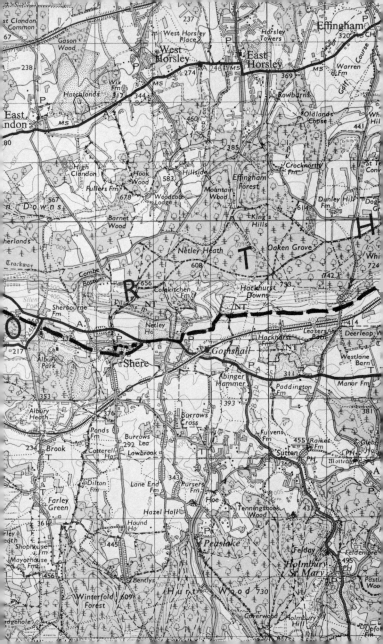

cathedral dominating Stag Hill to the west of the
town. It is a long way to walk, by way of Farnham
Road, turning first right up Guildford Park Road to
Stag Hill, and is perhaps best reached by taking the
Aldershot & District bus on route 27.

Travellers will come to this impressive building in a
hundred or a thousand years' time just as we now
come from Winchester to Canterbury. The cathedral
is built in the shape of a cross to Sir Edward Maufe's
design, and from end to end measures 365 feet. It is
70 feet high and 40 feet wide, and the top of the
tower is 180 feet above the ground.

The main vaulting is of concrete, sprayed with
asbestos plaster to prevent echoes, and externally
faced with rose-red coloured bricks. You will have to
decide for yourself whether you approve of this
Neo-Gothic compromise, but it is the proportions of
mass, volume, space and line rather than elaboration
and the repetition of ornament that make this cathedral so imposing. The foundation stone was laid by
the Archbishop of Canterbury on 22 July 1936, and
rests on stones brought from the fabric of both
Canterbury and Winchester Cathedrals. The cathedral
was completed and consecrated in 1962.

Guildford to St Martha's 2 miles

Cross the river at St Catherine's Ferry and on the far
side continue along a clear grassy path across a
meadow to the road A281 from Guildford. East of
the main road take Pilgrims' Way Road, which after a
few hundred yards bends left into Echo Pit Road.
Here a private drive forks right, signposted to Chantries and St Martha's, which can be followed by
vehicles.

Bear left at whitewashed Chantry Cottage and
enter into the fringe of Chantries Wood, passing soon
South Warren Farm on the left. Continue on the

Guildhall and High Street, Guildford

track through the wood, then fenced between fields, shortly to enter the wood again. Here the main track bends sharply left to emerge at the road by Tyting Farm. Where the track bends there is a rustic seat and two notice boards and we take a path continuing in a forward direction to emerge at Half Penny Lane, a few hundred yards south of Tyting Farm.

At this road turn left for a short distance, and at the 30 mph signs take a narrow path on your right leading up to the open heath, used as a car park for those visiting St Martha's. Keep the close-boarded fence on your right, and when this ends keep straight on up the hill. The old road is just discernible as a sunken way through the pines, but as it nears the summit it disappears, only to reappear some 20 yards or so at the beginning of the descent on the other side.

On the isolated summit of this high ridge stands the famous little church known as St Martha's on the Hill. It has become, rather inconveniently, the parish church of Chilworth, a hamlet of modern bungalows in the valley below where from Elizabeth I's reign until quite recently banknotes were made.

St Martha's stands 573 feet above sea-level with a glorious view over the wooded Surrey countryside. It stands at a place where, almost certainly, heathen worship was practised by the Early Bronze Age people who lived on this hill, and it is thought also to mark the place of massacre of early Christian martyrs. Some say the church is dedicated to St Martha because she actually visited this spot when, in company with Lazarus and St Joseph of Arimathea, she visited Britain. There is no other church in England dedicated to St Martha.

The church is constructed of Burgate ironstone with sandstone dressings; materials from the hill on which it stands—an isolated summit of ironstone surrounded by sandstone of a geological fault. The

church was in ruins until it was rebuilt in 1850 in the
impressive Norman style on its original cruciform
foundations and with a low central tower. It contains
a minimum of carved detail, but has a window in the
south wall of the chancel dedicated to St Thomas
Martyr and bearing the Arms of Canterbury.

St Martha's stirs the imagination, yet there is only
a brief outline of its history on record. It became one
of the possessions of Newark Priory, a few miles
away, before Magna Carta. When Edward I and his
queen were away in the Holy Land candles were lit
here for their little son Henry lying ill in Guildford
Castle. In the reign of Edward IV Bishop Waynflete
of Winchester granted Forty Days' Indulgence to any
penitent who made a pilgrimage here or gave money
for the upkeep of the church. In his document, dated
20 May 1463, the church is called 'the chapel dedicated to Saint Martha the Virgin and all the Holy
Martyrs commonly called Martirhill'.

After the monasteries were dissolved St Martha's
came into the hands of the squire of Chilworth
Manor, and it gradually fell into ruin as the genera-
tions came and went. Roofless and neglected, but
with services still being held in the chancel, it had
become a sorry sight until it was rebuilt. The church
is open all Bank Holidays and every afternoon except
Monday during the period April to October.

St Martha's to Shere 3 miles

We leave St Martha's by a gate in the churchyard wall
at the eastern end and pass by a clump of pines. At
the foot of these trees can be seen the sunken trackway again, overgrown with gorse and bracken, and
not used by today's pilgrims who prefer to use the
sandy paths on either side. An old wartime pill-box
stands on its line at the fringe of the trees, and the
depression of the old track can be followed to a
prominent yew tree, then to the Albury-Guildford

The Pilgrims' Way on the Ascent to St Martha's

road called Guildford Lane. We will come to see several of these wartime defensive structures in the next few miles, but whether by coincidence or design they all seem to be sited on the line of the Pilgrims' Way, and they therefore help to define the route we must follow.

Go through the gate on the opposite side of Guildford Lane and into a field and bear right along the edge of the field to a tubular steel gate in the far right-hand corner. Continue along the top edge of the next field with a wire fence on your right to a wicket gate at the corner of a wood, then once more along the top of another field, with a fence on your left down to a gate leading into a hedged lane which serves Newbarn Farm. Pass through the iron field gate immediately opposite and bear slightly right uphill across the field to a wicket gate at the corner of a wood. Pass through this into the wood, and with the wood on your right and the field over the hedge on your left drop down to Water Lane leading north from Albury up to Newlands Corner.

Here arises a difficulty unique in the whole course of the Way. The trail for once goes to the damp and northward side of a hill, upon which stands Weston Wood. Turn left up Water Lane for 20 yards, then right past two pairs of semi-detached houses along a grassy lane, sunken between hedges, to pass north of Weston Wood.

One hundred yards or so past a little cottage, by a prominent chestnut tree on the left, bear half-right along a sunken track, with a row of beech trees on your right, to emerge at the corner of the wood in a clearing. Albury sand pit lies concealed in the trees on the right and the track on the left leads past a timber yard to the main road A25.

Cross the track to the sand pit and climb a stile ahead, bearing right round the edge of the wood to another stile, then bear left beside a barbed-wire

St Martha's Chapel
108

fence to a stile at the main road A248, just south of its junction with A25.

Just to the north of this road junction is the famous Silent Pool, reputed to be haunted by a beautiful maiden who was drowned in the pool many centuries ago. If you come on a moonlit night you may see her bathing, and if you keep still and quiet you may hear her shriek as she disappears below the surface of the still waters.

Albury lies just south of the Way in the gentle
Tillingbourne valley, a picturesque estate village of
the 1850s. The village was bodily transplanted from
its old site in the Park in the early nineteenth century
to this location ½ mile westwards, the site of a hamlet
then called Weston Street. Pretty cottages cluster
around the Romanesque church of St Peter and St
Paul, built of brick in 1842 in a style that would
hardly be out of place on the Italian Lakes.

To the east of the village and the main road A248
is Albury Park, home of Her Grace Helen Duchess of
Northumberland, GCVO, CBE. Unfortunately the
house, gardens and park are not open to the public.

Just south of the Pilgrims' Way beside the main
road is the spectacular Irvingate Church, a surprising
sight among the trees. Edward Irving created a great
sensation in London by his preachings and prophecies
and was later tried for heresy. He came to Albury and
his enthusiastic friend Henry Drummond built this
church for him at a cost of £16,000 in 1840. The
interior has some handsome woodcarving by a local
man, the best of which is the very beautiful altar
made of cedar wood brought from the Holy Land.
The church is no longer used for services, but a key
may be obtained from the caretaker in the adjoining
bungalow.

Cross the road A248 and take the track opposite
past the caretaker's cottage, over a stile and straight
ahead through a field to a field gate and stile at the
edge of a wood. Here the Pilgrims' Way gains a prominent ridge, from which one may gain occasional
glimpses of Albury House through the trees.

The original house was Tudor, half-timbered, but
was almost entirely rebuilt for the Duke of Norfolk in
the seventeenth century. The house was altered
c.1700 and then again c.1800 and was finally completed and depressingly remodelled in 1846-52. Architecturally it now has little to offer except an

unconvincing Tudor Style, with brick dressings to the windows, battlements and gables, and a set of sixty-three ornate brick chimneys culled from every imaginable Tudor source, each one different.

Historically the main interest in Albury is the landscaped garden, laid out by diarist John Evelyn and George Evelyn from 1655 to 1658, chiefly in parallel terraces along the side of the hill north of the house and below the ridge carrying the Pilgrim's Way. A grotto was excavated under the main terrace and a tunnel, which still exists, was built right through the hill.

The old Church of St Peter and St Paul in the Park near the house can just be recognised by its shingled

The Irvingate Church, Albury

dome to the tower peeping above the trees. The
church was disused from 1842 when the new one was
built in the estate village of Weston Street. In the
chapel lies Henry Drummond, who bought Albury in
1819, the politician and banker who helped found
the Catholic Apostolic Church with Edward Irving.

When you enter the wood take the higher, left-
hand footpath to the crest of the ridge where some
tree felling has taken place. Keep to the right along
the ridge, descending to the edge of the wood at an
iron kissing-gate. Pass through the field to another
similar gate straight ahead, and drop down to a metalled lane. Cross this and take a footpath directly
opposite, which soon leads to a road. Turn right in
this, crossing over the Tilling Bourne ford by a footbridge, then bear left into the village of Shere.

Shere is a pretty little village, having drawn many
an artist to paint the quaintness of its narrow picturesque streets and colourwashed cottages. The old grey
Church of St James add much to the delight of the
scene and is found at the end of a funnel of cottages
forming Church Square on the south side of the
Tilling Bourne stream.

The church has an early Norman central tower
topped by a big shingled broach spire dating from
about 1275. There are two fine doorways: the south
having a Norman arch richly carved with chevrons
and foliage, and with several mass-clocks scratched
below it. The west doorway is thirteenth century and
beautifully moulded, framing a big studded door of
1626. There are several beautiful windows containing
fragments of fourteenth-century glass, and the best
remains show the symbols of the Evangelists:
Matthew's angel, Mark's lion, Luke's bull and John's
eagle. The east window of 1902 is an effective mosaic
of colour, particularly when seen from a distance.
There are several fifteenth-century brasses, four in the
south aisle and two in the chancel. Also in the south

Church of St James, Shere

aisle is a case displaying woodwind instruments used
in the minstrel gallery during the early nineteenth
century.

Shere to Dorking 7 miles

The Pilgrims' Way may have passed beside the southern porch of the church, and if it did it would have to
cross the Tilling Bourne again, and this double
crossing of the stream may be accounted for by the
presence of a shrine and of a settlement in the oldest
times. If the road bridge be taken as an indication of
the original place where the stream was recrossed,
however, then the track would have left the church
on the right, and would have turned round to become
the present Dorking Road leading to A25.

The map in the bus shelter on the Dorking Road in
the village shows the Pilgrims' Way leaving Shere
church by a path leading to the south-west corner of
Gomshall, then just east of the railway bridge over
A25, having crossed the Tilling Bourne and Gomshall
Marsh. It is then shown making a right-angled left
turn up Beggars Lane, under the railway again, and on
to Hackhurst Downs. This right-angled turn has been
made for no possible reason and this line cannot but
be a confusion with the old drover road to London.

From Shere the track must have crossed the high
road A25 at a point nearly opposite Netley House,
and by a slow climb made for the flank of the Downs
and the chalk, and followed this line until it reaches
Chilham, some 65 miles away.

Beyond the grounds of Netley House and just
before you enter Gomshall take a road on the left
signposted 'No Through Road for Motor Vehicles' and
after a few hundred yards take a signposted footpath
on the right. The old road is lost here, but it must
have turned gradually eastwards to cross the mouth of
Coalkitchen Coombe, which here runs into the hills,

and have reached in this fashion the 400-foot contour at the corner of Hackhurst Downs near a pill-box, on the edge of National Trust property.

From this point the line of the Pilgrims' Way can be followed for miles without undue difficulty. Its platform is nearly always distinct, and the line is marked by yew trees, though the platform is cut here and there by later roads. Box Hill attracts and holds the eye as one looks eastwards, a hill prominent in the landscape of the Downs.

Three hundred yards beyond the pill-box the path crosses Beggars Lane which comes up from under the railway arch at Gomshall. The path continues straight along the 450-foot contour above a wood, and the sunken pathway can be observed, overgrown, immediately on the right. In ½ mile a good footpath comes up from Hackhurst Farm and soon enters a sunken path, bordered by yew trees. Immediately on the left by the start is an old chalk quarry guarded by a wartime pill-box, but although this path leads plainly north-east up to a height of 700 feet it heads too high up the hill for it to be the old road, which follows a less noticeable path at about the 475-foot contour. This barely discernible path lies just above the field hedgerows and emerges by another chalk pit as a distinctly sunken track at the apex of a hairpin of the road which leads up steeply over the Downs to Effingham.

Follow the road downhill for a short way, and when it turns sharply right continue ahead along the 450-foot contour past an old quarry. Keep the quarry on your left and follow a belt of trees on your right, then across an open ploughed field to a track leading up from Park Farm. Do not follow this track uphill, but contour round a thickly wooded coombe, Pickett's Hole, past old brick buildings of a disused rifle range to a path leading up from Coomb Farm.

Follow the top edge of a cultivated field, with

woodland over the wire fence on your left. The old
road is over this fence, overgrown by hawthorn and
bramble, but after a while you may enter the wood
and follow a narrow path. Soon you meet a larger
path coming in from the left which you follow ahead,
and when this bears left continue ahead on a narrow
path to emerge at the edge of the wood by a wicket
gate. Go through this along the lower edge of a field
with a wire fence on your right, coming soon to the
apex of a hairpin bend of a muddy track. Turn up
this track and pass through a gate, then along a
delightful semi-metalled track becoming a metalled
drive which gradually drops down in 2 miles to a

White Downs

Ranmore Church

lodge at the Dorking road below Ranmore Common.

The spire of St Barnabas' on Ranmore Common is a landmark for miles, but it is doubtful if the track of the Pilgrims' Way passed over Ranmore Common. Undoubtedly a prehistoric track led over that heath, but it was a branch track leading to the Thames. Presumably the old road followed a spur down the shoulder of the hill to the River Mole, but the actual line is lost in the ploughed land of the valley.

When the Dorking-Ranmore road is reached continue downhill to the entry to the Dorking Lime Works. Housing estate roads must be followed as the original line is lost; cross the road and pass along Limeway Terrace, left into Chalk Pit Lane, right along Yew Tree Road and into Keppe Road. This footpath leads down to Calvert Road and across a footbridge over a railway cutting to the A24 London Road.

The line of the Pilgrims' Way reappears on the lower slopes of Box Hill across the river, but we must leave the exploration of the next section for the following day after we have seen Dorking, an old market town situated on the River Mole where it breaks through the Downs.

Dorking

Dorking is an excellent centre for walking, and was at one time noted for its edible snails. The town obtained the grant of a weekly market in the reign of Edward I, and today its ancient inns, winding High Street, raised causeway and bow-fronted shops give a strong feeling of its original character.

Left: The North Downs from the slopes of Box Hill, looking west
Pages 120-121: Polesden Lacey Manor near Dorking

6

Part three River Mole to River Darent

Dorking to Merstham 9 miles

It has been argued that the Pilgrims' Way crossed the Mole at Burford Bridge, 2 miles north of Dorking. Burford suggests a river crossing, and possibly pilgrims may have crossed the Mole over stepping-stones and contoured round the western flank of Box Hill, but this route would have taken early travellers far out of their way—a diversion of 3 miles rather than a direct 1½ miles between the two known points on either side of the Dorking Gap.

The name Burford suggests a ford, but the Mole is unlike other streams south of the Thames in that it 'swallows' and 'burrows' underground, and at any one of these 'swallows' the river could quite easily be crossed. Perhaps no other stream in England has attracted so many poets: Spenser wrote of it in his 'Faerie Queene' as

'Mole, that like a nousling mole doth make
His way still underground, till Thames he overtake'.

Milton called it 'sullen Mole, that runneth underneath', and Pope, in his 'Windsor Forest' mentions the 'sullen Mole, that hides his diving flood'.

Whenever, in crossing a valley, the old road diverges from its general alignment, it does so either to avoid bad soil or to find a ford. It always chooses a place where some spur of high land leads down to the

The Crossing of the River Mole below Box Hill

river and corresponds to a dry rise immediately
opposite upon the other bank, but at Burford, on the
western side, there is quite a little plain which must
have been marshy. Burford Bridge was in fact built in
connection with the Stane Street Roman Road which
runs north-south through the Dorking Gap.

Box Hill

Many people will wish to continue along the ridge
over Box Hill, and those doing so will find it best to
take the wide chalky footpath just north of the Burford Bridge Hotel. The hotel, formerly known as the
'Fox and Hounds', was where Nelson bade farewell to
Lady Hamilton before Trafalgar, and here also
stayed Keats and Stevenson. It is said that Keats
found his inspirations for the last 500 lines of 'Endy-
mion' on Box Hill, and in a letter to a friend he tells
how he went up the hill by moonlight and came
down with some of these lines in his thoughts.

Box Hill is a beauty spot with the usual attendant
car parks and rustic cafes, and every day in summer
modern trippers from London and all the country
round flock to the top of the hill for its famous view.
It is not one of the most extensive views, but from
this noted viewpoint, 590 feet above sea-level, we can
look down and across the Weald and wide expanses of
countryside. Far beyond the blue-green haze is Ash-
down Forest and the backs of the South Downs,
while nearer at hand is the landmark of Leith Hill,
965 feet, and at our feet the shining River Mole winding to the Thames.

The hill is densely wooded not only with box trees
from which it gets its name—some of the finest in
England—but also with juniper and yew, and in spring
and summer the whitebeams show finely among their
deeper green and those of oaks and beeches.

Pages 128-129: The North Downs from below White Downs,
looking east

Dorking to Pebble Coombe 3 miles

From Denbies on Ranmore Common, then, it is probable that the old road went east down the spur past the chalk pits to the valley, crossed the railway just north of Pixham Mill. It would then ascend the hill before it to that spot where it distinctly reappears on the 300-foot contour line just west of the lane leading up to Boxhurst and the crest of the hills from the Reigate Road, A25.

The Pilgrims' Way cannot be followed until Boxhurst is reached, so from A24 we must take a lane on the right ¼ mile north of the junction of B2038, which leads down to some stepping-stones across the Mole. If the river is in flood it can be crossed by a footbridge a few yards downstream. A path rises and falls as it crosses the lower slopes of Box Hill among the trees, but it follows just above the level of cultivation and soon reaches Boxhurst.

Beyond Boxhurst follow the line of electricity pylons at the top, left, side of a field, soon coming to a pill-box at the corner of a wood, Brocken Warren Wood. Here the Pilgrims' Way appears distinctly as a terraced track lined by yew trees. Follow a stately but abandoned avenue along the bottom edge of this wood and after a while you drop down to Brockham Chalk Pits and old lime workings. An interesting time can be spent looking at the old and overgrown kilns, and a collection of old narrow gauge steam locomotives and railway stock, but we must follow a small gauge railway on our right for a few yards only, then bear left along a footpath. When the great Betchworth Pit is reached, which forms an impasse across our route, turn up steeply left to a muddy footpath on a higher level, which crosses the workings by a narrow brick bridge, and so down to a row of cottages. Pass these and bear right along a lane leading to the road B2032 leading from Betchworth to Pebble Coombe.

The chalk hills between the Mole and the Medway

Ranmore Church

Box Hill

Buckland Hills

have had many bites taken out of them by man, and many of them have cut into and destroyed the old road. The chalk would have furnished the flints which were the first tools and weapons of primitive man, but it is now necessary for the building of roads and the making of lime for soil dressing. As the old road was originally the only track along these hills, it was necessarily the base of every chalk pit that was dug. Later, when valley roads were developed and the old road was no longer continually used it was profitable to sink the pits deeper, below the level of the old road, as far as the point where the chalk comes to mix with the sand or clay of the lower strata. As the old road became more and more neglected the obligation of protecting it was forgotten, and the commercial exploitation of the chalk pits destroyed the road at these several points. The pits therefore afford a guide to the line of the old road in the few cases where it is lost.

Pebble Coombe to Colley Hill 2 miles

The old road crosses straight across the mouth of Pebble Coombe, and assumes a character of some perplexity. The escarpment of the hills here is very steep, so steep that it could not support a terraced road without such engineering works as primitive man would have been incapable of performing, and this steep scarp slope continues for some 4 miles to Quarry Hill above Reigate.

If the road could not be supported upon the bank of the escarpment, and yet desired—as it always must —to escape the damp land of the lower levels, it was bound to seek the crest. Nowhere hitherto has the road attempted the summits of the hills, but here it is going to keep to them as long as the steepness of the escarpment lasts.

It is possible that the Pilgrims' Way passed over the spur of Brockham Hill before reaching the Pebble

Retrospect from Colley Hill

Coombe road at height 353 feet, but if it did its line
cannot be traced or followed. Climb the Pebblehill
Road to a point just past three or four houses after a
series of bends in the road where a footpath turns
off east to the site of Bridlecombe Bungalow. A line
of yews can be seen in the woodland up to the left
above the field, indicating the climb of the old road
across the hillside from height 535 feet to a height
of 600 feet along the ridge.

At the end of this path turn left on a bridleway up
to the crest of Lady Hill and at the top cross over a
bridlepath in a steep-sided cutting coming up from
Underhill Farm. Do not descend, but turn right between yews along the 600-foot contour on the ridge.
When the wood ends follow a barbed-wire fence
between two fields to another wood ahead, and
follow the path round the south side of this with
another field on your right.

The gables and chimneys of a large whitewashed

Dorking   White Downs   Betchworth Pit

house, Mount Hill are now in sight, and we soon pass
this on our right hand. Cross the drive to this house
to a footpath opposite along the crest of the Buckland Hills. The path becomes very muddy under
laurel bushes to emerge at the gates of Juniper Hill on
the edge of the famous Walton Heath Golf Course.
Here bear left, then after a few yards turn right, to
the north of Swiss Cottage. Note the sunken way on
the right of the bridleway, an extremely muddy path
much churned up by horses hooves, which leads us
out to the open grass slopes of Colley Hill at the
corner of Margery Wood.

Colley Hill to Reigate Hill 1 mile

The track following the crest of the Buckland Hills,
Colley Hill and Reigate Hill is much overgrown, and
most of it, though quite plainly marked, cannot be
seen until you are right upon it. One has to stoop and
brush aside the branches of the dense undergrowth,
and all the track is damp and muddy, shaded from
the sun by the mass of old yews, and less well drained
on this flat top of the summit than it is on the hillside
where it usually hangs. Though it is a difficult 2 miles
to follow, the sunken track is plain to see, broad and
unmistakable .

The bridleway continues to be so muddy that it
is best to come out on to the windswept slopes of
Colley Hill, a magnificent stretch of open ground
with wonderful views over to Reigate and Gatwick
Airport far below. The sunken way can be clearly
seen to the north of the bridleway in the fringes of
Margery Wood. The path continues past an ugly brick
water tower to an ornamental drinking fountain and
public toilets on Reigate Hill, (both now non-function-
ing).

A good track leads east of Reigate Hill through a
wood, passing a vague area of unidentifiable military
property on the right and a concrete water tower and

At Brockham Pits
133

a steel radio mast on the left. These masts, buildings,
bunkers and chain link are an eyesore when seen close
at hand, yet to do them justice these towerscape
installations do not seriously mar the thickly wooded
skyline.

The boundary to the military property is marked
by a stone 'WD↑No.13' on its east face, and on its
north face 'War Department Boundary is the Northern Edge of Pilgrims' Way'. The track leads past a few
houses and WD post No. 14 similarly inscribed, then
drops down to the A217 Reigate road.

Reigate

Down to the right lies Reigate, an ancient town which
has become a popular residential and commuting
area. The town has been imagined to take its name
from the old road, but it lies too far below in the
valley to be connected with its passage. Pilgrims must
have come down to this point to sleep as they came
down to many other places along the route. So
common a halting-place was Reigate in the Middle
Ages that at the centre of the town, where the town
hall now stands, there was a chapel of St Thomas
from perhaps the thirteenth century to the Reformation.

Reigate Hill to Merstham 3 miles

A footbridge carries the Pilgrims' Way over a deep
cutting at the summit of the London Road A217, to
a place where car park, toilets and snack bar have
been provided at a viewpoint over the Weald. Once
across this road the Way points straight to Gatton
Park and the lodge on its far side.

Cross the road A217 and bear left past the car
park toilets and refreshment hut, then right to a road
called Gatton Bottom. This coincides with the Way as
far as Tower Lodge to Gatton Park, and here the Way

Water tower at Colley Hill
135

enters a wood north of the Hall and is marked by a terrace and an avenue of trees pointing towards the thatched East Lodge. The Way cannot be followed through the Park, but a public footpath passes close to it through the grounds.

Gatton Park is a 558-acre estate with a house and church, though the former was burnt down in 1934 to be replaced by a new house which is now the Royal Alexandra and Albert School.

The little fifteenth-century Church of St Andrew's is a mainly Renaissance structure and contains old treasures from all over Europe. It was lavishly decorated in 1830 by the fifth Lord Monson, who lived in the house at that time and looks more like the choir of a cathedral than the interior of a village church. Elaborate stalls from a Benedictine monastery in Ghent, Belgium, face into the nave, and many have misericords carved with faces. Looking down on them from a height is a rich pulpit, dating from about

Colley Hill   **Reigate Hill**

Above: Colley Hill and Reigate Hill from Reigate Heath

1530, which with the carved panels in the altar is
probably Flemish. There are carved doors from
Rouen and altar rails from Tongres, and the windows
have sixteenth-century Flemish glass from a church
near Louvain. All round the nave are delicate trace-
ried panels, leading up to a beautiful English Gothic
screen beneath the gallery at the western end. The
west window shows the arms of Henry VII.

From the East Lodge of Gatton the Way follows a
road for a short distance, then south of Whitehall
Farm along a track past a nursery garden; when this
ends continue on a footpath which goes gently down
the ridge of the falling crest. The public footpath
leaves the line of the old road, which passes through
the grounds and south of The Glade House at the top
of Quality Street to just south of Merstham church.
This line cannot be followed, so we must take the footpath coming out at Home Farm at a corner of A27 at
the south end of Quality Street. Here turn left to the
end of Quality Street and take a path on the right-
hand side beside The Forge to cross the M25 South
Orbital motorway by a new footbridge and to emerge
at Merstham church.

Merstham

In medieval days the quarries at Merstham were
famous for their sandstone, for it was used in 1259
for the King's palace at Westminster Abbey and a
century later for Windsor Castle. It was used for old
St Paul's and old London Bridge and many other
public buildings. Like many quarry villages, Merstham
has little architectural evidence of its own product,
except the church and the unexpectedly pretty
Quality Street.

Quality Street was so named because the leading
actors playing in Barrie's 'Quality Street' were living
here at that time, in an ensemble 1600-1700 buildings
of stone, brick, timber and tile-hanging with trim
front gardens. In complete contrast to this bit of the

Page 137: The Pilgrims' Way, Margery Wood, Colley Hill

Church of St Andrew, Gatton Park

139

Church of St Katherine, Merstham

original village is a depressing estate out in the 'green belt', a malignant growth dating from the 1950s to the east of the main road and railways. The faults of this, and other, dull housing estates could, perhaps, be overlooked if they were not so uniformly bad in their architecture. The sheer monotony of it all is depressing in the extreme.

The Church of St Katherine's was built on the wealth of the stone quarries in 1220 to the north of the village on the slope of the Downs. It has two fifteenth-century chapels with some original glass, while at the top of the tower arch is a carved heraldic stone which came from the old London Bridge. The lych-gate is said to be made from the oak timbers of an old mill which was pulled down when the railways came this way.

Another railway memory lingers in the empty cutting with a little bridge beside the 'Jolliffe Arms' on the Brighton Road to the north of the church. It is a relic of the first public railway in England, the Surrey Iron Railway, operated with horses from 1805 to 1838. It was used chiefly to carry the stone and lime from Merstham to Wandsworth for Thames shipment. Part of the track and its stone sleepers can still be seen.

7 **Merstham to Otford** 17 miles

Merstham to Gravelly Hill 3 miles

White Hill, Quarry Hangers and Gravelly Hill lie to
the east of Merstham, forming an extremely steep
escarpment, and it would be obvious that the old
road would be forced to take to the crest. The hills
have a number of steep ridges with spurs and inter-
vening hollows, and these would have made it
impossible for men and animals to go at a level halfway up the hillside. The old road, then, would have
to gain the crest of these Downs before their steepness had developed.

The pilgrims in the Middle Ages probably went
straight up the hill from Merstham by an existing
track to the ridge. It would climb the hill at a slant,
keeping to the chalk till it should reach the summit at
some point where the clay had stopped and the slope
below had begun to be steep.

East of Merstham church the old road is lost
among the confusion of the road A23 and the two
railway cuttings, but from along the lane on the
400-foot contour, Rockshaw Road, can be seen the
line of a hedge running diagonally and climbing slow-
ly to the crest. The Greystone Lime Works afford
another clue to the line of the road which is now lost.

From Merstham, then, turn east along Rockshaw

Road, which begins just south of and almost opposite the church across the main road. Follow this road over the railway cuttings for ½ mile and opposite a house called 'Noddyshall' on the right turn left along a grassy path, signposted 'Bridleway', beside two new bungalows, and follow this down the field to a gate leading to a sub-way under the M23 motorway.

Follow the farm track, go through a gate and continue your direction diagonally across a sloping grass field, through a little wood to a large swing gate. If you look back from this point a continuous line of yews can be seen coming straight from Merstham church and right across the old lime pit. Ahead, the track continues to climb the face of the hill to an iron field gate in the far corner at the top of the next field. Pass through the gate and turn right along a clear hedged track all the way past height 662 feet to the Chaldon-Bletchingley road.

One mile down the road from this junction with Pilgrim Lane is the lovely church of Chaldon, which contains a unique thirteenth-century wall painting showing the torment and punishment of the wicked and, on the upper section, the salvation of souls.

Cross the road into a lane opposite at Hilltop Farm, which after a while becomes a beautiful track, passing the W.T. station on your left, through a rubbish dump, to Willey Farm. Keep the main farm buildings on your right, and after 20 yards or so, at a fork, take the bridleway bearing to the right to the summit of White Hill Tower at the Stanstead Road junction. Turn right along the road for a short distance, then straight ahead along War Coppice Road, passing to the north of Arthur's Seat, the spur on which stands a prehistoric camp. A most beautifully wooded road keeps along the high ridge bending and dipping for ½ mile until the crossing of Weald Way. One hundred yards or so beyond this road junction bear right along a broad path, a distinct terraceway

143

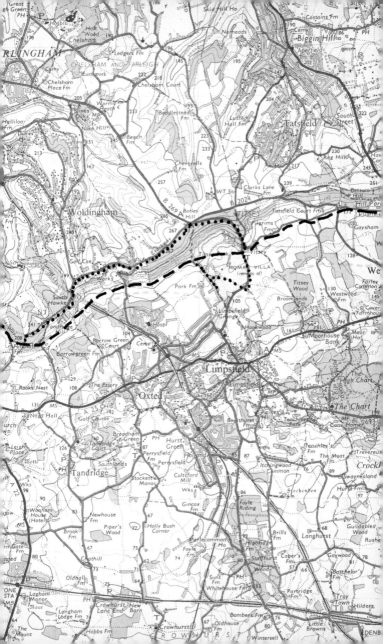

on the spur of Gravelly Hill. Horses have cut up the
surface of this chalky path rather badly, and it may
be easier to use a parallel path a little lower down, to
emerge in about ½ mile on the grassy slopes of the
famous Viewpoint.

The panorama from this ridge of Gravelly Hill
stretches over the Weald from Tunbridge Wells in the
east to Leith Hill in the west, with the South Downs
forming the skyline.

Gravelly Hill to Titsey 6 miles

To the east of Gravelly Hill runs a long deep coombe,
which may be called Caterham Coombe, up which
runs one of the two Roman roads from the south and
the modern London-Eastbourne road A22. On the
steep western side of this coombe the old road is lost
in the difficult undergrowth of Upwood Scrubs. It is
probable that the old road went round the outer side
of the hill 774 feet high rather than cross north of its
summit, but all traces of evidence have been destroyed. The probable line can best be followed by
taking the bridleway east of the Viewpoint contour-
ing round the spur of the hill, through the remnants
of an old quarry and a rubbish dump to a road
called Tupwood Lane.

Turn right in this road to a gypsy caravan site and
to A22 Godstone Road, which runs in a deep cutting.
The line of the old road cannot be easily found on
the other side, so cross the new footbridge over the
dual carriageway, and into the field ahead. Turn south
on a grassy track, the old Roman road, then turn left
on a track doubling back past Quarry Farm to the
Surrey Timber Company's Quarry Saw Mills sited in
the disused Godstone Quarry.

Just south on A22 at the crossing of A25 lies the

Quality Street, Merstham

village of Godstone, with a large central green and a
duck pond ringed by limes and chestnuts. The name
of the village is probably derived from the 'good'
limestone that was once quarried here and used for
the paving of Westminster Hall. Later, when the
Wealden iron-smelling industry spread to Godstone a
gunpowder mill was founded in the village by Sir
John Evelyn, and the quarries declined.

One mile north of the centre of Godstone we
rejoin the old road at Godstone Quarry and turn right
along a track skirting below Winders Hill. This lane is
called Flower Lane and follows the 600-foot contour
round the hill. It passes the lodge of Marden Park and
within a few hundred yards comes to a road above
Flinthall Farm at the apex of a hairpin corner.

Turn left along this road reaching a height of 683
feet, and when the road bends left again continue

ahead along a path below the plantation of Hanging
Wood, coming soon to a bend in another road which
leads up to Tandridge Hill. From this point onwards
for the next 3 miles the old road again takes to rough
ground, though its line cannot be followed by any
definitive public footpath.

Cross over the Tandridge Hill road to an iron field
gate opposite. Pass through this and through three
fields with a hedge on your right to a wire fence, no
stile, and a path coming up from Oxted. Turn right
and go down this path for a few yards then climb the
wire fence on your left, no stile, along the top of a
field below Rye Wood. Pass some old quarries and a
smallholding and across a field to a deep cutting
which is the entrance to Oxted railway tunnel.

Beyond the railway tunnel follow a fence and a
hedge on your left past an open barn and around the
next field, through a gap in the hedge and across the
next field to a field gate at the Oxted road. Cross the
road and pass through the field gate opposite and
follow a wire fence on your right to another gate at
the far end of the field. Keep a wire fence on your
right through another field leading to Limpsfield
Lodge Farm, an attractive 1700 tile-hung building on
the edge of Titsey Park.

Across the private grounds of Titsey Park the track
of the old road is clear, and passes just south of the
site where the old church once stood. The country
house of Titsey Place was built in 1775, but the
external appearance is stuccoed Gothic of 1832. In
the grounds was discovered and excavated in 1864 a
Roman villa, dating from AD 166-80 and measuring
130 feet by 55 feet.

Titsey to Chevening 5 miles

Titsey is a small village, little more than a few estate
cottages on the edge of the park. The Church of St

James was built in 1861 and has a shingled broach spire.

For the last 30 miles the route we have been following has consisted mainly of rough tracks, bridleways, footpaths or no paths at all, and has sometimes been hard to find, yet east of Titsey the old road is well defined and often metalled for much of the way, making it easier to follow.

Half a mile east of Titsey the Way passes Pilgrims' Farm and after another mile leaves Surrey and enters Kent at the crossing of the Westerham road B2024. At this cross-roads the Kent County Council have erected a sign with which one is to become increasingly familiar along the next 50 miles of the route—a plate bearing the lettering 'Pilgrims' Way' together with the symbol of the cockle or scallop shell of St James of Compostella in Spain. These signposts have been erected on the line of the route where it has been

The Pilgrims' Way east of Merstham

149

established beyond dispute, and sometimes also when
it is in doubt.

East of the county boundary the left-hand side of
the road is lined with builders' allsorts and wirescape,
and after ¾ mile of this we come to the crossing of
the main road from London to Westerham, the
A233.

A mile or so to the south on the edge of the greensand ridge stands Westerham, a pleasant and unspoiled old market town. Its well-kept green is
dominated by the statue of General Wolfe, the victor
of Quebec in 1759. His house, Quebec House, is
National Trust property and is open as a museum.

East of the main road A233 the Pilgrims' Way
continues as a metalled road past a lane to Pilgrims'
Farm and after another mile comes to a cross-roads
below Hogtrough Hill, where the lane climbs the
Downs from Brasted to Cudham. After another mile
and a half we come to the fence of Chevening Park,
where, by virtue of an Enclosure Act in 1785, the
route is barred to all traffic.

Chevening

The finely wooded grounds of Chevening Park are not
open to the public, and the traveller has to make a
detour north then south-east, partly through the Park
and partly on a newly created footpath to regain the
line of the Pilgrims' Way at the church of St Botolph
in the hamlet of Chevening.

The great mansion of Chevening has its main front
facing north towards the heights of the Downs. The
central block was built between 1616-1630 to a design
by Inigo Jones for Richard Lennard, 13th Earl Dacre.
After the death in 1715 of Lennard's grandson,
15th Baron Dacre, the estate was sold in 1717 for
£28,000 (in 24 yearly instalments of £1176) to James
Stanhope, one of Marlborough's generals. Stanhope,

Water tower at Gravelly Hill
151

now created the first Lord Stanhope, made extensive
additions to his new home. The original block was
extended to the east and west and the great entrance
forecourt was brought into being by flanking wings
joined to the central block by single-storey quadrants.

Had the great building so remained it would have
ranked as one of the finest early Georgian mansions in
England, but the 3rd Earl Stanhope changed its out-
ward appearance drastically by refacing it in stone and
cream-coloured tiles.

In 1959 James Richard, 7th Earl Stanhope, gave
his 3,500-acre estate to the nation, with an endowment
of £250,000 for the upkeep of the mansion. It was
his wish that it be used, following his death, by a
Prime Minister of the day, or a Cabinet Minister, or a
member of the Royal Family. The Earl died in 1967
and an Act enshrines his wish in law.

The original choice of occupant by Edward Heath,
then Conservative Prime Minister, was Anthony
Barber, then Chancellor of the Exchequer, and this
nomination would have resulted in him joining the
exclusive ranks of the Prime Minister and the Foreign
Secretary in having his own official country home.
However, when it was realised that the new occupant
would have to pay tax in respect of residence there,
Mr Barber had to decline the offer.

A special Act of Parliament was needed to over-
come the tax problem, but then as Mr Barber felt that
it would be wrong for him to benefit from his own
legislation, the House then offered it to the Lord
Chancellor, Lord Hailsham. He lived at Chevening for
just six months, until the defeat of the Conservative
government in February 1974.

After Lord Hailsham's departure there was much
speculation as to who would occupy the house.
Lord Stanhope had not wished that the house be
occupied "by a succession of ministers" although it
seemed that the likely choice would be a senior mini-

Church of St James, Titsey

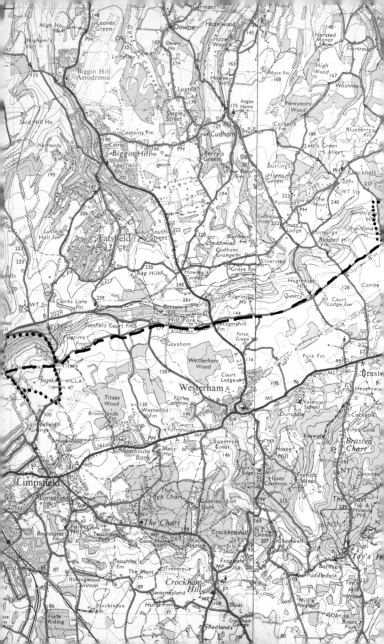

ster in Harold Wilson's Labour government. However,
with such a slender majority in Parliament, the
Prime Minister was obviously unwilling to commit
someone to taking up a house which he might have to
leave at short notice, and instead the house went to
the Crown.

In May 1974 it was announced in Parliament that
H.R.H. The Prince of Wales, Prince Charles, had
agreed to make Chevening his country house, thereby
quashing rumours that he had declined an earlier
offer because of his commitment to the Royal Navy.

The mansion has undergone extensive renovations
since 1970, lasting four years and exhausting the
endowment fund. The stone facings and cream-
coloured tiles were removed, the brickwork restored,
the fourth floor and flat roof removed and a new
hipped roof, similar to the original, was built in its
place. These extensive structural repairs won Chevening
a place on a list of schemes of exceptional merit in a
nationwide competition organised by the Civic Trust
to coincide with European Architectural Heritage
Year, 1975.

In the parish Church of St Botolph standing hard
by the main gates of the Park are a number of the
tombs of the Stanhopes and the Lennards. If the
church is locked, the key may be abtained from one
of the cottages opposite the lych-gate.

The church had Norman beginnings, but has been
greatly restored and altered. The long and narrow
thirteenth-century nave has its arches on round piers,
while the western tower is a characteristic example of
the fifteenth century. The altar frontal has the Tudor
rose and crown of England in blue on a gold ground,
having been made from a piece of the fabric which
covered the stands in Westminster Abbey at the coronation of George VI.

It is held that St Botolph was a favourite dedi-
cation where travellers and pilgrims gathered. A St

Church of St Botolph, Chevening
157

Botolph's church often stood at the gate of a city to welcome wayfarers, and it is said that there was once a St Botolph's at each gate of London. The one at Bishopsgate is a classic example of this association, and another stands at Aldgate.

Chevening to Otford 3 miles

The hamlet of Chevening stands just outside the Park and the road that leads up from Chipstead along the north-east edge of the Park stops by the church. It was used extensively for the transportation of fish from the coast about Rye to the London market, but it fell into disuse when the Park was enclosed in 1785.

The carriageway drive leading north from the main entrance of Chevening House crossed the Pilgrims' Way about 300 yards north of the house by a brick bridge; although the bridge was demolished in 1841

that part of the Park is still called Bridge Lawn. The
line of the Way passes along the northern boundary
of a field to a small wood behind Turvins Farm and
Morants Court Farm, then over what is now ploughed
land along the line of a hawthorn hedge and barbed-
wire fence until it strikes the byroad leading up to
Knockholt Pound from Dunton Green.

Here the Way leads straight to the crossing of the
River Darent down just such a spur as marked the
crossing of the Mole. After a short while we pass by a
chalk pit, and the road is stopped off at the entrance
to the works. At some bollards a few yards further on
we reach the main highway from London to Sevenoaks, A21, and the start of the Sevenoaks Bypass.
The road lies below the level of the Way, so descend
to the right to a gate, then go straight across the dual
carriageway to the continuation of the lane opposite.
Go along this lane, pass under a railway arch, down
the hill past some nondescript housing development

Above: A Pilgrims' Way sign as found in Kent
Left: The Pilgrims' Way at the Surrey/Kent County boundary
159

to the valley and a bridge over the River Darent and
into Otford.

Otford

From time immemorial the gap in the Downs through
which the Darent flows north to join the Thames has
formed a trunk artery of approach to the wide valley
lands of the Weald beyond. Between the railway and
the river lie the traditional sites of two great battles.
In 774 Offa, King of Mercia, fought and conquered
Aldric, King of Kent, and then in 1016 on a site ½
mile away Edmund Ironside had a great and success-
ful struggle with Canute and his Danes, inflicting a
crushing defeat upon them. Ironside followed his
beaten foe as far as the Medway crossing at Alresford,
when no doubt the Danish retreat was along the old
road.

Trackways of prehistoric origin followed along

each bank of the Darent from that other great trunk
route which became the Roman Watling Street to join
the old road. Many travellers from London bound for
East Kent chose to voyage down the Thames to Dartford or Greenwich and then follow the Darent to
Otford in preference to riding along Watling Street,
and then east along the old road. This was the choice
of King Henry VIII on his way to France and the
Field of the Cloth of Gold on 21 May 1520.

Today the Darent crossing at Otford is quite
unspectacular. There is no attractive bridge and one is
barely conscious of any river crossing at all. The road
continues eastwards to the junction of the Sevenoaks
road A225, which forms a roundabout around a most
attractive and well-kept pond, fed with water from
one of the many springs hereabouts. In the centre of
the village is the Church of St Bartholomew and
Archbishop Wareham's great Palace.

In 790 Offa gave land in the area to Christ Church,

Canterbury, and soon after the Norman Conquest
Lanfranc arranged that the property of Christ Church
should be divided between the Monastery and the
Archbishopric. The manor of Otford fell to the latter
and the power of the See of Canterbury and allegi-
ance to the Archbishop became a strong influence.

The archbishops made Otford one of their places
of residence—the medieval church could boast a
chain of palaces from London to Canterbury, but
they were more posting-houses than anything else. In
the days when the roads were dangerous and insecure
a small army of retainers, grooms and baggage porters
would have to accompany the Archbishop, his
messengers and guests from place to place on a
journey to and fro between Canterbury and London.
They demanded stabling, entertainment and food,
and the so-called palaces were necessary to keep up
the communications of the church life in those rough
days. With the exception of Maidstone, all the palaces—Otford, Wrotham, Maidstone and Charing—
stood directly upon the old road and are now in
ruins. They were the chief centres of Kent south of
the Downs, but they were destroyed by the new
landlords of the Reformation and now lie forgotten.

Archbishop Wareham, prelate between 1503 and
1532, demolished the early manor house and at a
present-day cost of £250,000 built the imposing
palace, the fragmentary remains of which today bear
witness to the ostentatious splendour customary
among the late medieval church dignitaries.

The palace measured some 440 feet by 220 feet
and was two storeys high with tall towers at its
corners, and some idea of its appearance may be
gained from the existing ruin of the north-west angle
tower. The whole must have been a typical example
of Tudor architecture; red-brick walls built in Old
English Bond enlivened by a diamond pattern of
purple headers, stone dressings to plinth, quoins and

Pages 160-161: Chevening House

Otford Palace

163

Church of St Bartholomew, Otford
164

windows, tiled roofs and probably a forest of grace-
fully twisted chimneys rising from massive stacks.

Today in addition to the ruined tower, the only
remains are the walls of the adjoining row of cottages
fashioned from one of the original galleries.

The palace passed to Cranmer on Wareham's death
and he was host to Henry VIII when he stayed here
on his way to France with his retinue of 4,000, plus
1,000 attending his Queen Katherine. Whether his
lavish entertainment here and the delights of
Wrotham and Charing made Henry envious of the
Archbishop's country palaces we do not know, but
Cranmer handed them all over when Henry appointed
himself Head of the Church of England.

Henry soon tired of the palace and turned it into a
residence for Princess Mary. Under Edward VI the
lead was stripped from the roof and the house soon
began to fall into decay. The palace and its domain
remained with the Crown until the time of Elizabeth,
but the queen sold it in 1601 to raise money to
finance the Irish Expedition.

Today the tower has its roof open to the sky, with
birds flying in at its windows and plants growing in its
crannies, a poor neglected building and a pitiful sight.

Just north of the old palace and facing the village
green is the Church of St Bartholomew, with a
timbered porch dating from 1637 leading into a
squat, square, battlemented Norman tower, capped
by a shingle spire. The new timbered porch leading
into the nave was erected to mark the Silver Jubilee
of George V in 1935, and bears an elegant little coat
of arms. A fire in 1635 caused serious damage to the
church, which was mainly repaired in brickwork, and
it was later drastically 'restored' in 1873 by the Victorian ecclesiastical architect Street.

From the churchyard a path leads towards the
railway station alongside a meadow, which contains
behind some tall iron railings on the right-hand side
Becket's Well.

The tradition concerning the origin of this spring is of considerable antiquity and Becket must have been familiar with the spot. The story is told that the Archbishop, in need for water close to the site of his building operations, and cursing the lack, struck the ground with his staff, whereupon water instantly flowed forth as it now does today. It has often been suggested, however, that the well was used in Roman times, and indeed, remains of a Roman villa have been found nearby.

There can be little or no doubt that this spring provided the only water supply at the time when the manor house was built. Excavations uncovered the massive stone lining of a great tank, measuring 36 feet by 19 feet, and covered by a timber roof. The formidable iron railings which surround the site prevent the visitor from inspecting the well at close quarters.

8

Part four River Darent to River Medway

Otford to Snodland 10 miles

Otford to Kemsing 2 miles

From the centre of Otford the old road passes to the
north of the church in the form of the road A225,
the main highway which runs through the Darent
valley connecting Dartford with Sevenoaks. Beyond
the railway station this main road bears sharply left,
and the Way continues ahead, bearing slightly right,
as a by-road passing beneath the shoulder of the
Downs.

Within the next six miles the old road exhibits
nearly all the points characteristic of its course, and
these permit us to deduce much that can be elsewhere
applied to the less-known sections of its course.

As throughout nearly the whole of its course
between Dorking and Chilham, the old road runs here
upon the bare hillside above the valley. The road
appears to run at the same level all along the hillside,
but in reality it is rising as the floor of the valley rises,
in order to keep continually at the same distance
above it.

These six miles may be divided into three nearly
equal parts to show the old road in each of its three
historical phases: first as the only artery of the
countryside, then as a way supplemented by a valley
road, and finally as a decayed and unused path whose

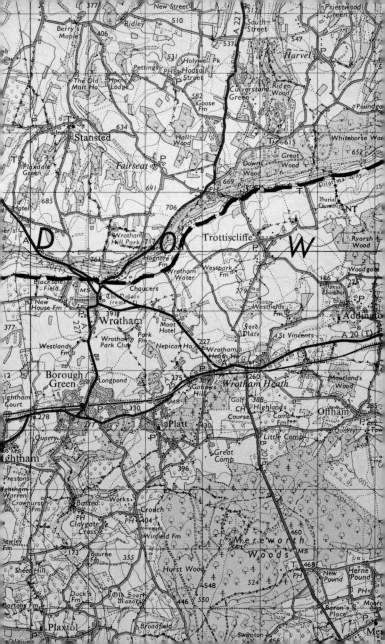

value has been destroyed by the alternative and more
modern road below it.

The first stage of the route from Otford to Kemsing is of a semi-urban character, where there must
have been a considerable amount of ribbon development during the interwar years. The road one follows
is the only good road between these two villages, but
it lies above them both, and the Way can only be
reached from either by a short rising lane. If you
desire to halt you have to leave the old road and
come down from it to the village below, exactly what
was done for centuries when the archbishops came up
to London from Canterbury.

A visit to the charming village of Kemsing involves
only a short descent, but is well worth the trouble. At
the crossroads in the centre of the village is a simple
war memorial cross standing above a spring, although
its stone-ringed head is now covered in. This spring is
St Edith's Well, which was named after the daughter
of the Saxon King Edgar. She was born in Kemsing in
961 and died twenty four years later, and the spring
later gained local fame for the curing of sore eyes.

Further to the east and a little way north of the
main village street is the snugly sheltered Church of St
Mary the Virgin, of Norman origin but greatly restored and enlarged during the 1890s. The church has a
shingled tower and turret and an interesting fourteenth-century porch, which leads us into a building
full of the work of ancient craftsmen, rich, beautiful
and colourful.

The lower part of the chancel screen was begun in
the fourteenth-century and the upper part, though
restored in 1894, is rich with carving. The painted
walls of the chancel are rich in colour and there is
delicate carving everywhere. The silver chalice is
exquisitely engraved by an Elizabethan craftsman,
and within the altar rails on the sanctuary floor is
perhaps the oldest priest brass in the country—a

demi-effigy of the rector of Kemsing from 1341 to
1347. There is a brass to another vicar on the chancel
floor.

The altar canopy is a magnificent sight, covered
with twenty-five shields on which are painted the
thirty pieces of silver, the crown of thorns, and all the
other emblems of the Passion. On each side are niches
in which are shown the Kings paying homage to the
Child, and Our Lord transfigured in the clouds. The
coats of arms decorating the chancel walls are of local
families.

In the south wall is an Early English single lancet
window dating from 1220 and containing perhaps the
oldest glass in the country: a medallion of a Mother
and Child. There are fragments of fifteenth-century
glass in other windows, whilst that behind the altar
shows Christ enthroned in majesty.

During the Middle Ages a shrine to St Edith stood
to the south in the churchyard and was once a place
of special devotion to the pilgrims and others who
had been cured at her Well. It was destroyed during
the Reformation.

A private drive leads up beside the churchyard to
an imposing building which was once the vicarage. It
is now a popularly-used youth hostel, and the Pilgrims' Way passes its gates.

Kemsing to Wrotham 3 miles

Beyond Kemsing the Pilgrims' Way becomes a pleasant country lane lined by banks with hedges and
trees. The 2 miles to the grounds of St Clere show the
second stage in the history of the road, for modern
influences have provided an alternative. The Way runs
along the hillside as a metalled lane, while below the
old footpaths and cart-tracks have been united into a
modern road, and a man going this way need not take

to the old road above, but go straight along the lower
level through Crowdleham and Heaverham.

The charming Stuart period mansion of St Clere
was built during the reign of Charles I, in 1631 or
1632, for Sir John Sedley. It has finely proportioned
elevations crowned by boldy massed chimney stacks
above tiled roofs, and it can be seen from the roadside in its parkland setting.

Between St Clere and Wrotham is the section
showing the final stage of the road, for here the more
common condition of modern times asserts itself. The
lower valley road now becomes the only important
one, passing the Tudor house of Yaldham Manor; the
old road dwindles first into a lane very little used and
falling into decay, then as a path thick with brambles
and almost impassable.

From St Clere the higher road is followed between
hedges for ½ mile to where it turns right. The Way
becomes a track once more, and we continue below
the boldly rising escarpment of Wrotham Hill. Here a
tall BBC mast with VHF transmitter erected on the
crest comes into view, a prominent landmark, being
typically characteristic of an age which decorates its
landscape with gigantic electricity pylons and other
similar monstrosities.

We follow this lovely track between the hedges
and under great trees below the slope of the hill to a
road coming up from Ightham. Cross this road and
continue straight on again for another mile along the
beautifully hedged track between orchards, coming
soon to a road at a corner. Continue ahead along this
road to the crossing of the Old London Road, A20.
Go over this main road and continue along the lane
for a few hundred yards to the Wrotham Bypass, then
again along the lane ahead for 200 yards to the Gravesend Road, A227. Here we may break our journey by
turning right to a roundabout, then down High Street
and into Wrotham.

Wrotham

Wrotham is an old village with russet roofs situated at
the foot of the hill where ancient roads met. Merci-
fully it has been spared the rush and roar of the
ceaseless motor traffic passing on the main London
road immediately to the north. The famous motor
and motor-cycle track of Brands Hatch is not so far
away and on race weekends all roads in the area
should be avoided. At these times home-bound
motorists race along the narrow country lanes in
souped-up family saloons, intent on emulating their
idols on the track and avoiding the inevitable traffic
jams.

The earlier Archbishops of Canterbury selected
Wrotham for the site of one of their several palaces,
which here provided a mid-way resting-place between
Otford and Charing. The palace was demolished
almost entirely by Archbishop Islip (1349-66) to
provide material for his larger palace at Maidstone.
Any remains which may be seen are now in the
private gardens of a house behind the church.

The parish Church of St George in the centre of
the village is of quite outstanding interest, and has
one very peculiar and puzzling feature; an arch going
through the base of the massive fifteenth-century
western tower which rises hard against the highway.
This vaulted passage, a rarity in England, was provided to enable the Sunday procession before High
Mass in medieval times to circle the church without
leaving consecrated ground. This performance would
otherwise have been impossible, but as the road was
there before the church, why did the architect build
right up to the road and then have to pierce his
masonry to allow a passage round the building?

The bold south porch is a great two-storey affair
with an angel in its vaulted roof and a bronze St
George at the door. The upper chamber is reached by

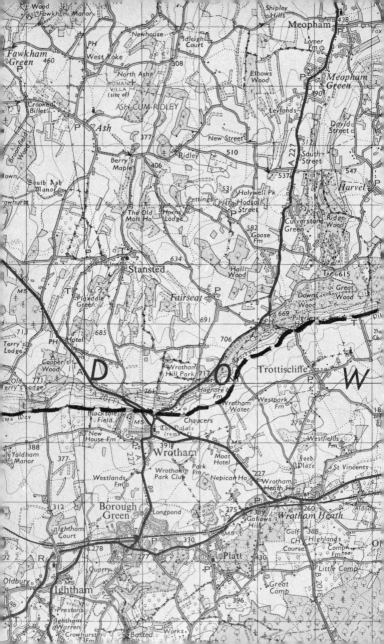

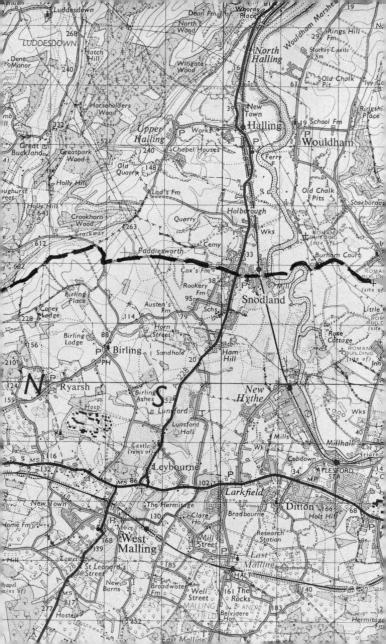

Church of St George, Wrotham

a curious stair-turret covered by a 'pepper-pot' roof.
The earliest work in the church now remaining is the
thirteenth-century nave arcading, but in the main
Perpendicular period details prevail; the large fifteenth-century windows, for example, have replaced
the older styles, and there are more modern ones
showing the Shepherds and the Kings at Bethlehem.

A curious fifteenth-century newel staircase,
approached from the east end of the south aisle, gave
access to the rood-loft, long disappeared, and continued upwards to above the apex of the chancel arch
into a nun's gallery in the north roof by a tiny
passage. This passage is lit by three small windows or
peepholes, two looking into the nave and one into the
chancel. The church is particularly rich in brasses,
having a remarkable portrait gallery with about fifty
figures of five families, and ranging in date from 1498
to 1615.

Wrotham to Snodland 5 miles

We rejoin the Pilgrims' Way at Wrotham a few yards
beyond the roundabout along the Gravesend Road,
A227. Cross this main road to a metalled lane
opposite marked by the usual KCC sign, and follow
this narrow road for a little over a mile along the
450-foot contour. All along this stretch are magnificent views over the wonderful valley spread out
below. Across the Medway valley can be seen the
distant heights of the Downs above Boxley and
beyond to Charing Hill.

After a while the metalled road bends sharply right
to Wrotham Water, but you keep straight on along a
clear track ahead. After 25 yards or so fork right on a
hedgerow path, much overgrown, later widening into
a grassy track, and follow this for ½ mile or so until
you reach a road coming up from Trottiscliffe to the
Gravesend road A227 at the 'Vigo Inn'. The 'Vigo Inn'
belonged to a veteran who had fought with Admiral

Rooke at Vigo Bay and who spent his savings on
buying a pub.

Turn right at this road and descend the hill
slightly, passing on the left a charming old building
called Pilgrim House, which was once an inn called
the 'Kentish Drovers'.

Once more a village, lying in the shelter of the
Downs but ½ mile below the Way, tempts us to break
our journey. Trottiscliffe, or 'Trosley' as it is known
locally, is a quiet place of some charm grouped
around the junction of several lanes. An attractive
weatherboarded house near the centre of the village is
the home of one of the greatest of our modern paint-
ers, Graham Sutherland. The village has an interesting
church standing beside a large and handsome farmhouse which is the site of a palace once belonging to
the bishops of Rochester. These two buildings lie
beside the road about ½ mile east of the 'centre' of
the village.

The Church of St Peter and St Paul is small and
unusual, a little museum containing many interesting
features. The ground was given by Offa, King of
Mercia, to the See of Rochester in AD 788. In 1100
Bishop Gundulph built the chancel in the Early
Norman style upon Saxon foundations, and these
walls and windows remain today as the best-preserved
Norman walls in Kent. The nave was built about 1140
and the bold tower, serving also as a porch, was built
in the fourteenth-century. The tower walls are 4 feet
thick at the base, but taper thinner as they rise in
height. The buttresses were probably added in the
early sixteenth century when other repairs were
carried out.

The most beautiful possession of the church is the
colossal pulpit brought from Westminster Abbey,
elegant, delicately carved, with a beautiful canopy,
and supported on a graceful branching pillar. The
pulpit was designed in 1781 and removed from the

Abbey in 1820 for the coronation of George IV. It was never re-erected, and probably without the knowlege of the Dean and Chapter it was given to Trottiscliffe church in 1824. About a hundred years later a farthing dated 1799 and a scrap of paper dated 1803 were found between the joints of the finial crowning the pulpit canopy.

The attractive communion rail dates from 1700 and an unusual feature is the small alms box built into the rail to the left of the gate. In front of the altar rail lies a local landowner and his wife, their tombs marked by two brasses dated 1843. The church choir was accompanied by a violin, tambourine and clarinet before the days of the barrel organ. The barrel organ was replaced in 1937 and is now in Rochester Museum, while the musical instruments are preserved in cases in the north wall of the nave. Some prehistoric remains discovered during excavations of the Coldrum Stones in 1910 were placed in a case in the porch in 1932, but they are poorly displayed.

Immediately to the west of the church is the Manor House, an eighteenth-century looking building overwhelmed by vast new asbestos farm sheds. The house stands on the site of the palace built about 1187 in the time of Bishop Gilbert de Glanville (1185–1214). After the Reformation the bishops of Rochester ceased to reside there, and it was finally sold by them in 1867.

As we have already strayed this far from the Pilgrims' Way to visit the village and church, our next objective will naturally be the Coldrum Stones, which lie ½ mile to the east of the church. For 300 yards there is a good road which then turns sharply left and continues north past some 'Assorted Ideal Homes' up the slope of the Downs. At this right-angled bend a notice board indicates the direction in which the Stones may be found. A track, sometimes very muddy, leads for a full ¼ mile to a car park, and the Stones lie less than 200 yards to the north beside the track.

The Coldrum Stones, or more properly the Coldrum Long Barrow, are the remains of a Neolithic burial chamber. They are today the property of the National Trust, given in 1926 as a memorial to the Kentish archaeologist and antiquary Benjamin Harrison (1837–1921), and a bronze plaque mounted on one of the stones near the path records this presentation.

Once the circle with the dolmen stood complete upon its raised knoll overlooking the Medway Gap—a circle of towering columns 160 feet in circumference. Now the eastern half of the knoll is gone, probably when chalk was being excavated or cut away when the road, now no more than a bridle path, was made. Half the circle has fallen down as a result, but four massive sarsens about 12 feet by 10 feet stand poised

Burham   Bluebell Hill

The Coldrum Stones, Trottiscliffe

on the brink. The remainder of the circle lie prone in a more or less regular arrangement on top of the knoll—fallen giants of almost equal size strewn across the slope. Even now in its ruined state the monument is impressive and its site, facing the wide river valley, striking.

The remains of twenty-two Neolithic people, together with some bones of the ox, deer, rabbit and fox ascribed to the period about 2000 BC were discovered here in 1910, and they are displayed in Trottiscliffe church.

The Coldrum Stones is a complex megalithic tomb and one of a remarkable group of dolmens found in this part of the Medway valley, between Wrotham and Boxley, described as the 'Kentish Stonehenge'. These structures were all of Neolithic origin and were, without exception, burial places. The great stones are all sarsens, and are comprised of sand hardened into masses by silica infiltration, the presence of iron often resulting in a yellow-brown staining. The stones are not of any composition quarried locally, and it is possible that they were strewn about during the ice age and collected together to be erected for this purpose.

We may return to the Pilgrims' Way at Pilgrim House by retracing our steps through the village, or turn north on the bridleway past the Coldrum Stones up to the Downs. Alternatively we may take the road northwards past a rash of architect-designed houses—complete with imitation sandstone and plastic gnome-scape, and such imaginative and evocative names as Dawn, Stand-e-ze, Windrush, Hacienda, Bonavista, The Bungalow and Seven—to reach the Way below Great Wood.

Returning to the Pilgrims' Way at Pilgrim House, we resume our journey eastwards along the upper of two tracks, a poor surfaced road leading for nearly a mile along the 400-foot contour past some isolated

ribbon development. This stretch of the old road is in
the nature of a terraceway, having been cut out of the
hillside to form quite a considerable drop to the
south. We soon come to a road junction a little way
above a telephone kiosk, an unexpected but convenient amenity in this isolated spot, and from this point
we may descend to visit Trottiscliffe church and the
Coldrum Stones if we have not already done so. A
little over ¼ mile east of the telephone kiosk the hard
road ends (turn right here down a bridleway to visit
the Coldrum Stones) and the way once more becomes
a terraced track between hedges.

This trackway is quite unspoilt, running green and
straight for two miles below Whitehorse Wood, and a
delight to walk upon. It is enclosed for the most part
by hedgerows and in places is overgrown, but one
cannot fail to see a brick-built 'thing' on the left after
one mile or the gentle views on the right across the
long narrow valley of Holmesdale.

When you reach the Birling-Vigo-Meopham road a
track ahead is signposted 'Pilgrims' Way' but ignore
this and turn right, passing an overgrown chalk pit on
your left, and keep on down the road for about
¼ mile and then turn left on the road through Paddlesworth to Snodland and the Medway.

From this point above Paddlesworth is a wide
prospect between two spurs of the Downs across the
wide and tidal Medway. Much of the view is industrial, but distance here lends a peculiar enchantment
to this unlovely scene. The new Medway bridge can
sometimes be seen, a slim, mile-long thread built in
1963 to bypass the Medway Towns, with the silver
towers of Grain Refinery catching the sun beyond.
The gaunt cliffs of quarries at Halling and the long
hangars of Rochester Airport on the opposing hill are
often the limit of our view, as the smoke and dirt
from paper mills and cement factories blot out the
middle distance.

From a distance Paddlesworth appears as a text-book example of a primitive community settlement, but the buildings lose much of their charm at close range, being dominated by electricity pylons and large asbestos sheds. There is a fine red-brick farmhouse and great barns on one side of the road in a state of dereliction and a small Norman church on the other. The tiny church was deserted at the time of the Black Death and has been used as a barn for a long time, but at least it has been saved from becoming a complete ruin.

From Paddlesworth continue eastwards on the road down Constitution Hill to the main Rochester-Tonbridge road, A228, in the centre of Snodland, a depressing industrial village with cement works and paper mills. The less said about Snodland the better. It contains all the kinds of ugly housing produced in this country during the last fifty years, and even the Norman Church of All Saints contains little of interest.

Cross the main road and continue down High Street and over the railway line by Snodland station, then by Mill Lane to the south of All Saints Church, where a footpath leads to the bank of the River Medway. Medway mud is, almost without reservation, noxious; the flats revealed here when the river is low are evil-smelling and repulsive, and one's enjoyment of the scene will depend on the state of the tide.

Part five The Medway Crossing

The River Medway was the largest and most serious
obstacle to pilgrims following the old road and it
poses one of the biggest problems concerning the line
of the Way.

At Wrotham the chalk cliffs turn away from their
general line and reveal the wide Medway plain at your
feet, but far off they continue their interminable line.
Along those hills our way is clearly to be continued.
Their trend is not due east, but they turn a little
southerly, and the furthest visible height is not far
distant from our goal.

On the far side of the valley the Pilgrims' Way is
recognised again, but in the interval between, across
the broad flat valley, its passage has never been fixed.
In so wide a gap as here made by the Medway a great
difficulty arises, greater than any yet met. It is too
easy to assume that the old road crosses in a straight
line and a longer search would be necessary to find
the true crossing-place of the river.

Far up the valley on each escarpment are the
remnants of an ancient road, and as in the valleys of
the Mole and Darent, difficulties increase because of
other prehistoric tracks leading off northwards upon
either side of the river.

The great main ridge of the chalk escarpment of
the North Downs affords for 60 miles a platform for
the Pilgrims' Way, but here at the Medway it is

broken, for it turns north to form a 'funnel'. The
interval between these hills, a distance of some 6
miles, is the most considerable of any on our journey.
Had there been no physical obstacles to intervene, the
first travellers upon this track would have undoubtedly made a direct line from the projecting shoulder
of Wrotham Hill to the somewhat less conspicuous
turning-point of Bluebell Hill. But serious obstacles
do intervene: a broad river with swift tidal current,
flanked here and there by marshes, and a valley floor
of clay, the crossing of which must prove far more
lengthy and arduous than that of any hitherto encountered.

Oddly enough, the difficulty of rediscovering the
original track by which the pilgrims crossed the
Medway does not lie in the lack of evidence, but
rather in the confusion arising from possible alternatives. In crossing such a major obstacle, and a tidal
one at that, a very strong reason for one single track
would be a valuable clue, for if one place of crossing
had held a monopoly or even a pre-eminence, the
evidence afforded by it would be of the utmost value;
but an indication of this simplicity is completely
lacking.

It is certain that the river has been crossed at four
places, each of which may now lay a claim to be the
original passage, and these places are Cuxton, Halling,
Snodland and Aylesford. Furthermore, the two tracks
of great antiquity on each side of the Medway are not
only clearly defined but have each been given the
traditional name of the Pilgrims' Way, and their
presence adds a considerable embarrassment to the
search for the original passage.

Let us now recall those certain features which we
have discovered to be true of the road in the earlier
part of its course where it had to cross a river, and
certain other features which one may add and conjecture that the road would possess:

1 The road will attempt the shortest passage of the valley floor, the breadth being less of an obstacle than the damp soil.

2 The road will seek a ford.

3 Other things being equal, it would naturally cross a river as high upstream as possible, where the stream was likely to be less difficult to ford.

4 It would cross as close as possible to that height upon which survey could be made of the valley floor.

5 The nature of the river bed at the crossing would influence it greatly, whether the bottom be gravel, sand or mud.

6 A point of so much importance would probably be connected with religion, and almost always with some relic of habitation or defence.

7 It would often preserve in its place-name some record of the crossing.

8 It would choose a place where a spur on either side led down to the river.

To these eight points may be added for further consideration:

9 That whatever was the more usual crossing in early times affords something of a guide as to prehistoric habits.

10 Where a tidal river is concerned, the motives which were present for seeking a passage as far upstream as possible would be greatly strengthened, for the tide drowns a ford.

In the light of these principles, let us consider Belloc's views on the subject as to where a crossing is most likely to be found, and having discovered that, examine how far this is supported by other evidence. We know that the Medway has been crossed at four places since prehistoric times, and we shall study each of these in turn.

1 Cuxton

At this, the farthest point downstream, the river
widens into a tidal estuary, though sheltered, with
hills and firm ground leading right down to the river
on either side. Ancient terraced trackways lead very
near to the point of a possible crossing and indicate
that traffic did go this far north, but they cannot be
followed clearly. There is a constant tradition that
the crossing of the river at this point by pilgrims was
common, and this is the one favoured by Kent
County Council. They have signposted the road
passing through Upper Halling to its junction with the
A228 at Cuxton, and the signposts next appear on
the Rochester Road between Wouldham and Burham.

However, there is nothing like a ford at this place.
The bottom is soft mud, the width of the river is very
considerable, the tidal current strong, and of all the
points at which the river might have been crossed, it
is the most distant from the direct line; indeed,
compared with the next point upstream, Lower
Halling, a traveller would add 5 or 6 miles to his
journey by crossing at this point.

2 Aylesford

This is the opposite extreme to Cuxton, being the
highest point upstream, and it has several points in its
favour. One of the strongest is that legend records a
retreat of the Saxons from a defeat at Otford by
Offa, King of Mercia, along some road to the Medway. Later the same thing happened when Ironside,
after his great victory over the Danes at Otford in
1016, pursued them to Aylesford, where he was
prevented from destroying them by their passage over
the river. The Pilgrims' Way would be a natural route
along which the defeated armies could make their
escape.

Aylesford also preserves the tradition of a ford in the last part of its name, though 'ford' in place-names by no means always signifies a ford, any more than 'bridge' signifies a bridge. In this case, however, we have historic knowledge that a ford existed, and, as is most frequently the case, the ford has been bridged, here by the finest medieval example remaining in south-east England. When this bridge came into being it is reasonable to suppose that vehicular traffic would have found this more convenient than to negotiate a ford, and have accepted the extra distance involved by diverging from the shortest line.

There are three strong arguments against these points, and one is that the valley is so wide, an immense tract of uncertain wooded land, as to give no view either of enemies or direction. Secondly, a belt of clay stretches all along the Downs just below the level of the chalk and here it is particularly wide. No straight line can be taken from Wrotham to the Aylesford gravels without crossing nearly 2 miles of this wretched footing which, throughout its course, the road has most carefully avoided. Thirdly, a number of prehistoric remains lie to the north of such a crossing, and in order to reach Boxley, a site undoubtedly dependent upon the prehistoric road, man would have to turn back upon his original and generally easterly direction. If Cuxton and Aylesford are to be discounted as being too far off the general line (as Belloc thinks they certainly must be), there remain only Halling and Snodland.

3 Halling

One might conclude that this was the original crossing of the Medway, for there was a good surface from the track on the hills above right down to the river bank at this point. No clay intervenes between the chalk and the gravel and one would have had fairly dry land

underfoot all the way down to the river. Even beyond
the river the belt of alluvial soil is less broad than it is
at Snodland, and if the geological argument alone
were to be considered, the decision would undoubtedly be given to this place.

4 Snodland

Claims are asserted for this crossing by a number of
points, individually slight but convincing on the
whole, and these must be examined in more detail:
1   The spur which leaves the main ridge of the hills
for the river (as at Shalford and Dorking, attracting
the Pilgrims' Way to it) touches both Snodland and
Halling on either side, but Snodland is on the south
and Halling on the north of the slight ridge. The
southern side would dry quicker in winter, and in a
dry summer it mattered little whether the slope be
partly of clay (as is the descent to Snodland) or of
chalk (as is that to Halling). During more than half
the year, therefore, the descent to Snodland was
preferable, and during the other half indifferent.
2   Antiquities are numerous in the locality of Snodland. An ancient chapel marks the descent from the
hills at Paddlesworth, while beyond the river a
Roman villa was unearthed in 1896 precisely upon
the road that would lead from such a crossing of the
Medway to the track upon the hill at Burham.
3   The crossing at Snodland is shallower than that at
Halling, and at this spot is a natural outcrop of greensand which has defied all dredging operations in the
past. A ferry no doubt adequately provided for the
needs of foot travellers in the Middle Ages, as in fact
it continued to do until quite recently, while those on
horseback would have had no difficulty in crossing
here by the ford at low tide.
4   There stands at Snodland a church, past the southern porch of which goes a road, and when the river is

crossed and the same alignment followed along the
bank upon the further side for a little way, the track
again passes by a church, and again by its southern
porch.

5   The 'Horseshoe Reach' of the Medway has always
marked the limit between Rochester's jurisdiction
over the lower, and Maidstone's over the upper
reaches of the river. This fact is of great importance.
All our tidal rivers have a sea-town and a land-town;
the limits up to which the seaport has control is
nearly always at the traditional crossing-place of the
river—London and the Thames has the best example
of all in Staines.

6   The megalithic monument of the Coldrum Stones
corresponds to that of Kit's Coty House on the
opposite shoulder beyond the valley. Both monuments are within sight of the old road, and this rela-
tive position may have something to do with the
alignment of the route through Snodland. There is a
tradition that an avenue of stones stretched from one
monument to the other and thus marked out a
crossing from one line of hills to the other in a zone
where the hillside is no longer a guide to the position
of the road. The river crossing at Snodland would be
a natural route between the two. The stones are now
gone, if ever they existed.

These converging lines of proof, or suggestion, would
seem to settle the discussion in the favour of Snodland, but in all probability these different crossings
were used from time to time as conditions of the river
bed and tidal water varied. It would be misleading to
point to any one spot as 'the' crossing.

9

Part six River Medway to River Stour

Snodland to Charing 16 miles

Snodland to Burham 1½ miles

It is unfortunate that the one-time ferry at Snodland
no longer operates. In the absence of any means of
crossing the Medway at this point the modern traveller is faced with a long detour before he can resume
his journey from the east bank. The nearest bridge
crossings are either by footpath beside the M2 Motorway near Rochester downstream or Aylesford upstream, and as Snodland lies midway between these
two points there is no difference in the choice of
either bridge.

If one choses the Aylesford crossing there is the
temptation to cut that section of the Way between
the river bank opposite Snodland and Bluebell Hill,
but in doing so one would miss a fine section of the
old road and a magnificent retrospective view of the
Medway as the gradual climb is made towards the
Downs.

It is, of course, possible, in fact probable, that the
river has during the centuries altered its course to
some extent and the great bend of the 'Horseshoe
Reach'—where the meander of the Medway doubles
back to within 100 yards of itself—may be very
different from what it was in medieval or prehistoric
times. Nevertheless, the site of the ferry which plies
no more represented a traditional crossing-place at
Snodland, the point where the old road strikes the

river bank having passed immediately south of the church. On the eastern shore an embankment runs round the bend until it reaches a spot close to Burham Court.

Scattered throughout the Burham marshland are the grim remains of disused lime kilns and cement works. Although many factories are in view, they are safely out of reach and the riverside is peaceful. The only sounds nearby are the rustle of the tall waving reeds screening the margins of the river and the 'kraak' of a tall grey heron disturbed from one of the numerous pools left by former industrial workings.

At Burham Court farm the river embankment runs into a made road which almost certainly must be part of the old road, and here the ancient parish Church of St Mary's stands hard against the farm buildings. This Norman edifice with a fifteenth-century western tower is now empty, deserted and in decay, for today a modern church serves the village a mile away. The church stands on ground just above the flood level of the river close to the crossing, a lone sentinel here in the marshes.

Beyond the churchyard the road begins the ascent gradually towards the foot of the downland scarp. It has all the characteristics of an early trackway, such as we can recognise in many places on this journey to Canterbury; the track or path raised above the fields on the south or right-hand side, and a steep bank on the left, the terrace thus formed having been cut or worn out from the sloping ground.

After a while we pass near to Burham village and there are magnificent views across the Medway, particularly towards Snodland with the great chalk scar of Holborough Knob showing brilliantly white against the green background of the Downs which extend as a skyline to Wrotham in the far distance. A graveyard of factories down on the marshes, evidence of the cement industry of the last century, is backed

by the paper mills at New Hythe and Snodland
beyond the fantastic contortions of the river. In the
evening sunlight, with the dusty smoke of the active
cement works drifting across the river, these shattered
ruins have an air of unreality.

Burham to Boxley 3 miles

Burham is an ugly village with an impressive Gothic-
revival church, beautifully set under the Downs. Close
to the roadside south of the village near Petts Farm a
Roman building was discovered during 1896.

Beyond the junction to Eccles the road becomes a
dual carriageway and rises gently towards Bluebell
Hill to reach the Aylesford road at a corner. No part
of Kent is so rich in prehistoric remains as the district
we are now approaching. There is the Coffin Stone at
Tottington and 500 yards to the east are the Countless Stones, Fallen Stones or Lower Kit's Coty House,

Burham Churches   Bluebell Hill

as they have variously been called. This latter group is now preserved as an ancient monument in common with the more imposing Upper Kit's Coty House.

A few hundred yards down the Aylesford road on the left-hand side and marked by a clump of elms, will be seen the group of fallen megaliths known as the Countless Stones (signposted Little Kit's Coty), the ruined burial chamber of a prehistoric long barrow. It is so called because it is said that no one has been able to number them correctly, or no two people arrive at the same answer when they try. There are not many of them and they are all in a heap, and it is difficult to know if two stones counted are really opposite ends of the same stone sticking out of the ground.

A little further to the south still, a track on the right-hand side of the Aylesford road leads between a hop field and an orchard to the Pilgrims' Spring, the Coffin Stone at Tottington Stone Circle.

Church of St Mary, Burham

Back at the Aylesford road and the junction of the
dual carriageway to Burham a signposted path leads
up between high hedgerows to Kit's Coty House, the
remains of which will be found in a field on the left.
These Neolithic remains consist of three upright
stones, 7-8 feet high, surmounted by a capstone
nearly 13 feet long. They formed the central com-
partment of the burial chamber and were once enclosed by an earthern mound covering, but this has
been completely eroded away. The Ministry in whose
care the monument now rests has, with quite remarkable insensitivity, thought fit to 'protect' it with a
hideous iron cage.

It is significant to note that both groups of monuments—Kit's Coty House and the Coldrum Stones—
are on prominent sites, although well below the
downland escarpment, with magnificent views down
upon the river and the whole extent of the Medway
Gap; approximately on the same level on the sides of
the valley; each visible from the other; and both
having another stone circle a short distance to the
south—here are the Countless Stones and on the other
side are the Addington Stones.

Both monuments are dolmens—i.e. two massive
upright stones raised to support a horizontal table-
stone. At Coldrum the table-stone has fallen, but at
Kit's Coty House the arrangement is complete. It is
the generally accepted opinion that these structures,
after internments had taken place beneath them, were
covered with mounds of earth, and around them was
placed a circle of standing or recumbent stones, such
a circle being termed a 'cromlech'.

For the traveller who is unable to recognise the
affinity between the monuments of Coldrum and
Kit's Coty House and, those of the Rhineland and the
Low Countries, and their dissimilarity to those of
Wiltshire, their principal appeal will lie in their vast
scale and in the splendour of their settings.

Pages 196-197: The River Medway at Snodland

After Kit's Coty House return to the Pilgrims' Way
and take the hedged and signposted path for ½ mile
to emerge beside the Rochester-Maidstone road
A229 just below a petrol filling station.

From the crossing of the A229 the old road pre-
sents little for comment, save that over the next 15
miles it is more direct, more conspicuously marked
and better preserved than in any other similar stretch
of its whole course. Nothing of its ancient character
has been lost: it is not a permanent road as is the
section between Alton and Farnham, but on the
other hand it is not—except in two very short places
—interfered with by cultivation or private enclosure.
This stretch of road is a model to scale, preserved
from modern changes and even from decay, but
exhibiting those examples of disuse which are characteristic of its history.

The road goes parallel to and above the line where
the sharp spring of the hills leaves the valley floor; it

commands a sufficient view of what lies ahead; it is
well on the chalk, just too high to interfere with
cultivation (or at least with the cultivation of those
lower levels to which the Middle Ages confined
themselves); it is well dried and drained by the south
slope and the porous soil; it is uninterrupted by
coombes or any jutting promontories, for the range
of the hills here is exactly even. In short, it here
possesses every character which may be regarded as
normal to the original trail from the west of England
to the Straits of Dover.

The villages which lie immediately below the Way
are all at much the same distance, and all but one lie
just to the south. These villages—Boxley, Detling,
Hollingbourne, Harrietsham, Lenham and Charing—
are now connected by the modern highway A20
which joins up the valley settlements which were
once, it may be presumed, isolated from each other
by the common fields of each village. They may have
depended for their intercommunication upon the old
road for many centuries, for each of them possesses a
definitely marked line of approach to it; the old road
remains the typical main artery, which passes near,
but not through, the places it serves.

The crossing of the Rochester—Maidstone highway
occurs some 600 yards below the 'Lower Bell' Inn. At
first the track appears to be no more than a wide footpath, but vehicles may get through in dry weather.

After some 250 yards the Way enters the fringe of
the large Westfield Wood, which covers all the downland to the north. Just beyond this point, if one looks
carefully, will be found another megalith, the White
Horse Stone. It is not easy to locate, particularly in
summer, when it is much obscured by the overhanging foliage, but in winter when the branches are
bare of leaves it is fairly obvious. It may be found by
a worn and narrow footpath leading up the bank on
the left-hand side.

Kits Coty

Like the coincidence of the Coldrum Stones and
Kit's Coty House, the coincidence of the name White
Horse Stone here and White Horse Wood above the
Coldrum Stones is significant.

For a while the Way passes through the fringes of
the wood to emerge on to the big open hillside, in
summer a spot beloved by picnickers. Here the
Downs rise for 600 feet or more, a level maintained as
far as Charing and beyond. Further on the woodland
again drops close to the Way at Boarley Scrubs and
we reach the road coming up from Sandling and
Boxley Abbey. At this point we must once more
break our journey, as so many other travellers must
have done, to visit the scanty remains of the once-
prosperous Boxley Abbey and the village of Boxley
itself.

The White Horse Stone

Boxley

A vast throng of devout and superstitious pilgrims
would have been drawn to Boxley Abbey to gaze
upon the supposedly miraculous Rood of Grace and
the figure of St Rumbold. This Cistercian Abbey was
founded by William de Ypres in 1146—one of the
earliest of the Order to be found in England—and was
destined to grow in importance and the wealth of its
possessions until it was unrivalled among the other
great monastic settlements of Kent. It was the Abbot
of Boxley who conducted the service over Becket
when they laid him in the crypt at Canterbury.

An enormous stone-built barn and stone walls
which enclose 15 acres of land are all that is left of
the abbey, which stood a mile south of the Way near
the village of Sandling.

The story of the Rood of Grace has aften been
told: how the monks acquired a figure of Christ fixed
to the cross from a craftsman, with an ingenious
mechanical device which enabled the figure to roll his
eyes and bow his head by means of a complex system
of concealed wires, and how for so long they imposed
on the ignorant its 'supernatural' properties, and how
it was eventually seized in 1539 by the King's
Commissioners and ignominiously burned before a
London crowd in St Paul's Churchyard.

The abbey was ruthlessly destroyed by Henry VIII
at the Dissolution. The abbey had been in his bad
books for some time, for it was here that the court
sat by order of the Pope under the presidency of
Cardinal Campeggio. The adjudicators were against
Henry's 'divorce' from Katherine, and the King must
have decided to have revenge some day, and his
charge was that the monastery had been wasting its
revenue by planting 'gillyflowers and roses' in the rich
soil of its grounds! The abbey met the same fate as all
the other monastic houses of the country, passing to

the Crown and subsequently by the King's grant into private hands.

Boxley village and its church lie about a mile to the east of the abbey and much nearer the Way. We must return to the point above Boarley farmhouse and resume our eastward journey. For the next 500 yards the old road is part of the road from Sandling to Bredhurst, and 500 yards further east at a signpost we drop down again to Boxley village.

Boxley is a small and quiet place beautifully situated near the foot of the steeply wooded Downs, from which issue several springs to feed a modest tributary of the Medway. The village has so far resisted development and takes its name, like Box Hill in Surrey, from the box trees that flourish on the Downs.

Boxley Abbey   Boxley churc

In 1840 Alfred Tennyson the poet came to live at
Park House and the fair countryside is featured in
many of his poems 'Prologue to the Princess', 'In
Memoriam', and many believe that one of the local
streams inspired him to write 'The Brook' in 1855:

> 'I steal by lawns and grassy plots,
> I slide by hazel covers;
> I move the sweet forget-me-nots
> That grow for happy lovers.'

As so often in Kent, it is as the focal point of a
delightful scene, rather than as a distinguished building in itself, that Boxley church is so valuable. There
is a charming village green and a pond, and by a group
of stately elms and an old yew stands the church of
St Mary the Virgin and All Saints. It exhibits work of
all periods, but its most striking feature is the unusual
narthex or chapel attached to the bold, Perpendicular
period west tower. Apparently this may once have
had a gallery from which sermons were preached or
relics shown to pilgrims. There are some fine decorated windows, particularly the one at the west end of
the north aisle, and there are two interesting brasses.
In the chancel is a monument with the family tree of
Sir Francis Wiat (1575–1644), Governor of Virginia
from 1621, who is buried in the church.

Boxley to Detling 1½ miles

The wooded hills above Boxley make a most beautiful skyline and there are little green rides from time
to time through the densely wooded slopes ascending
to the crown of the ridge. The chalk here is rich in
wild flowers, including some rare orchids. The woods
are largely of beech mixed with box, producing most
spectacular contrasts in colour at many seasons,
especially in autumn.

The Way becomes a tunnel of foliage below Box-

ley Warren and at the junction of Harpole Lane the
width increases and we come out at the foot of
Detling Hill where the main Maidstone-Sittingbourne
highway, A249, rises steeply to bypass Detling.

Cross the dual carriageway and after 50 yards or
so, round a slight bend, we see the jumbled roofs of
the 'Cock Horse' inn backed by a dense screen of great
trees. We now enter the village of Detling, where
immediately there are two features of interest. One
is the charming timbered house which stands immediately to the south of the Way and the other is a very
attractive old red-brick Tudor gateway that gives
access to the grounds of East Court, a mansion which
was demolished about 150 years ago.

Detling is a quiet hamlet grouped round the Norman church of St Martin of Tours. The church is not
a big one and architecturally is of no particular interest, except that the flint tower is capped by a helmet-
like broach spire which is of unusual pattern for
Kent. Let into the wall of the north aisle is a remarkable piece of stone, a 600-year-old carving of the face
of a man, with his hands clasped in prayer, but the
most striking possession is perhaps the oak lectern, a
remarkable fourteenth-century work which probably
came from Boxley Abbey. It has a beautifully carved
pedestal with four book-rests, the sloping sides of
which are enriched with period tracery of varied
pattern.

Detling to Hollingbourne 4 miles

From Detling the Way continues as a typical by-road
very little frequented, such as we have often encountered previously. To the north, as always, are the rising
heights of the Downs, while to the south lie orchards
and open arable fields, in summer golden with ripe-
ning corn.

After about a mile from Detling we come to a
cross-roads and the centre of the small village of

Thurnham, where stands Friars Place, a lovely half-
timbered and herringbone-brick house, built early this
century with fine ancient timbers. The church stands
a few hundred yards south of the 'Black Horse' down
the hill, but it possesses few features of particular
architectural interest to merit a special visit.

Three hundred feet above the village and just
below the ridge of the Downs are the ruins of a castle
once built and occupied by one Robert de Thurnham
in the reign of Henry II. When you get to the top of
the steep ascent after a perilous double bend and
when the lane has come out on to the level, you will
see a path through the trees to the right. Follow this
and you will emerge upon the ramparts of·the great
earthwork of Thurnham Castle.

The castle is a Norman defensive work of typical
motte and bailey type. The only fragments of masonry left are flint walls, some three feet thick, and these
are so hidden that it is difficult to find them among

the trees. The castle was built up and fashioned out of a natural spur of the Downs. To the south and east the position was defended naturally by the steep fall of the hillside, but its appearance has been much altered by chalk quarrying and by the deeply cut road on the west side. The entrenchments consist of a mound, more or less natural. To the north and west was a fosse, which with the passage of time has been nearly filled up, while a rampart was provided at the summit around the weaker sides. To the west of the mount a bailey or court was protected by a massive stone wall which may have been continued up the hillside to join one encircling the top.

It is probable that this castle was built upon the foundations of earlier structures to guard an ancient trackway over the ridge from Maidstone to the coast near Sittingbourne, a track used for the transport of salt. No doubt this castle, or fort, or watch-tower guarded the crossing of the two roads, and at a place that, on account of its position, was a good look-out station. From the castle summit the view over the Weald is magnificent and well repays the shortage of breath occasioned by the climb.

We rejoin the Pilgrims' Way below the castle in Thurnham and follow the road for a further 3 miles between hedges and open banks with the fields falling away gently to the south. We pass through the tiny hamlet of Broad Street and in a little over a mile we reach the Hollingbourne-Sittingbourne road, B2163, at the foot of the steep Hollingbourne Hill. If we turn right here into the centre of the village we will pass on our right Hollingbourne Manor. Only part of the great house, built in 1560, remains, but even so that which survives is a fine period building.

Hollingbourne is a small village nestling under the Downs. The green-treed hills provide the backcloth to red roofs, mellow brick and black-and-white timber-framed buildings which add much to the character

The Cock Horse Inn, Detling

and charm of the street architecture. The Perpendicular period Church of All Saints stands at the upper end of the straggling village in an attractive setting, and has several interesting features. There are three stained-glass windows in the south wall with pictures of Bible scenes and national saints: one with St George in gold, St Patrick in red and St Andrew in green; another with the Madonna, St Catherine and St Margaret; and another in the chancel with the Feast of Canaan and a scene of Abraham burying his wife.

The chapel is raised to the level of the altar and has 124 shields around its walls, but only two of them are decorated with coats of arms. There are many family memorials to the Culpeppers, who once lived at the Manor and once at Greenway Court, and the most notable tomb is that of Lady Elizabeth, who died in 1638. She lies, a life-size figure chiselled in white marble, with her head on a pillow and her feet resting on a most peculiar heraldic beast, vaguely dog-like but with large spots and cloven hooves. Lady Elizabeth's four daughters made the altar cloths for which Hollingbourne is famous, but they are exhibited only during the principal festivals of the church. These two magnificent pieces—hangings for the altar table and pulpit—are the most treasured possessions of the church, and represent thousands of hours of needlework stitched by the young ladies over a period of twelve years.

Hollingbourne to Lenham 3 miles

East of Hollingbourne the 'No Through Road' degenerates into a rough track. For the first few hundred yards this is surfaced and from the spot where this surfacing ends there is a fine prospect to the west of Hollingbourne church and manor with distant downland hills, blue in the distance where lies the Medway Gap. The next 2 miles or so is one of the finest

stretches of a grassy hedged track, a bridle path
sometimes skirting open meadows and arable land to
the south, at others passing below the tangled branches of trees and hedgerows.

The old road between Hollingbourne and Harrietsham was duplicated to the south by another and
possibly equally ancient track. Greenway Court
stands on its line at the end of the road one mile east
of Hollingbourne, and beyond it continues as a grass
path to Harrietsham church, becoming a road again
and forming the modern highway A20 to Charing.
This grass way was more generally called 'The Greenway'—hence Greenway Court—but in earlier times it
was known as the 'Welcumeweye'.

We come soon to a crossing road which descends
steeply towards Harrietsham, a village consisting of
two hamlets bisected by the arterial road A20 running between Maidstone and Canterbury. East Street
is the most attractive of the two parts of the village,
possessing a number of charming seventeenth-century
cottages, now mainly dressed up in Georgian frills,
and a group of almshouses built in 1642 by the
Worshipful Company of Fishmongers of London.

The parish Church of St John the Baptist stands
upon the line of the 'Greenway', away from the old
village but not yet submerged by the new. It is perhaps one of the most interesting and attractive along
this section of the route as it has, or had, two towers.
The original Norman church lay on the north side of
the present chancel and the remains of its west tower
now form a chamber above the vestry at the east end
of the north aisle of the present nave, which was built
in 1360.

The west tower of the present church was built
about 1480 and is an impressive and beautiful
example of its period. On the south side of the Early
English chancel is a chapel of 1320 which contains a
number of memorials to the Stede family, who lived

at Stede Hill on the crest above the village. The oldest
and best of the several tombs is that of Sir William
Stede, who died in 1574.

Immediately beyond the crossing of the steep
ascent from Harrietsham the Pilgrims' Way passes
south of the private grounds of the one-time home of
the Stede family, whose tombs we saw in the church
below. At the eastern boundary of Stede Hill Park the
Way resumes its normal character of a narrow by-
road. Even as late as 1810 it was recorded by the then
owner of Stede Hill that a 'Sheer Way' or 'Shire Way',
now called the Pilgrims' Way, was the only through
road from Hollingbourne to Charing.

In half a mile we come to Marley Court, a farmhouse with buildings of eighteenth-century character,
though perhaps now best distinguished by the odour
arising from the many poultry houses around it.
Opposite the farm, between the Pilgrims' Way and the
main road, spread the extensive buildings of a factory
manufacturing concrete roofing tiles. The shortage of
clay for roof tiles during the First World War led to
the introduction of the concrete variety, and the
Marley Tile Company is now world famous, turning
out a wide range of products.

Half a mile beyond Marley Court the Way once
more becomes a track when the road makes a right-
angled bend to the right, and we continue ahead for a
few hundred yards to join another road at a corner on
Lenham Hill. Follow this road for a few yards and
where it turns right we may follow it downhill to the
village of Lenham.

Lenham

Lenham was once a flourishing market town on the
old coach road, but it is now only a village bypassed
by the main Maidstone-Folkestone highway A20.
Henry III granted a market by charter and the

214

spacious market square indicates the importance of
the place when it was the agricultural centre for all
the surrounding countryside. On the north side,
screened by a row of lime trees, is a charming row of
old houses, some now converted into shops, while a
long, low inn, the 'Dog and Bear', occupies the west
side. There are several remarkable fifteenth and
sixteenth-century timber-framed buildings in the
village and some of these have Georgian or Early
Victorian shop fronts.

Lenham is on a watershed which causes streams to
drain west to the Medway and east to the Stour, but
the ridge is hardly discernible from the old road. The
watersheds of south-eastern England are low; the bold
ranges of the Downs do not divide the river-basins
because the water system is geologically older than
the chalk hills.

Lenham to Charing 3 miles

The Way leaves Lenham Hill as a tarmacked lane
leading past a big disused chalk-pit and a few houses,
then a field gate gives access to a fine stretch of
downland turf, in which is cut the great Lenham
Cross. This well-known landmark was established
immediately after the First World War and can be
seen from considerable distances to the south. An
iron railing at its foot once enclosed a granite block
recording the names of those who fell in the two
World Wars, but as it no longer serves its purpose it
ought to be removed.

Beyond the Cross we come to another field gate
and the Way now passes along a length of waste
bordered on either side by bushes and small trees. It
appears that this stretch is popular among gipsies and
tramps, judging by the number of soggy mattresses,
old campfires and other rubbish such as old pram
wheels and car seats, or it may be just another of the

many thousands of dumps which litter the roadsides and hedgerows of Britain. Fortunately we do not see too many of them along our journey.

For the next ¼ mile or so the Way becomes part of the Lenham-Warren Street road until it sweeps round some extensive chalk workings, then it continues as a track bordered by hedges for $\frac{1}{3}$ mile to the next crossing road. At the end of this short section are several houses occupied by staff of the Lenham Sanatorium. The Lenham Chest Hospital buildings form a prominent landmark on the crest above, from which can be seen a magnificent panorama over the Weald to the distant Channel horizon.

For 100 yards east of the road junction.the Way is a rough track, then for the next 300 yards or so it becomes a pleasant pathway alongside a field. It passes through a gate and beyond it the path narrows considerably, and is in the form of a terraceway raised 8 or 9 feet above the ground to the south. The path becomes very much overgrown, passes a row of tall pine trees, and it is only with the greatest difficulty that one can force a passage through to Cobham Farm.

Pass through a corner of the farmyard and take up the distinct line of the old road again passing between fields and through wicket gates to a concrete road at Hart Hill, ¾ mile further on. Beyond the first field the Way is tree lined similar to the other stretches we have found, then for the last 400 yards it crosses open pasture and arable land as a terraceway without hedges.

When the Way emerges on to Hart Hill it proceeds down the hill for a short distance, not directly across or up as has been its custom. Then, immediately below a house, it passes along the top of a deep dell much overgrown by trees. This may have been an ancient chalk working, but all signs have been covered in by soil washed down the hillside. Just above the

Way at this point is a prominent chalk pit, but it is no longer worked.

The spinney of trees on your right thins out and then the church tower and russet roofs of Charing village appear. We follow the tree-lined path for just over a mile towards Charing Hill, and soon the path leads us into a track passing a waterworks building and a few houses to reach the Canterbury road A252 by a tile-hung cottage. The Pilgrims' Way continues on the other side of the main road, but here let us turn right down A252, then left along B2077 into the centre of Charing village.

Charing is an attractive village which has long enjoyed the advantage of a bypass. It is situated at the fork of two main roads to the coast and the main village street is thus preserved from the worst of the horrors of through traffic. There are some good half-timbered and eighteenth-century houses in the main street, but hidden behind their facade is an estate of hideous concrete-panel utility houses, fortunately not noticed by the traveller on the Pilgrims' Way, but a regrettable and unfortunate foreground to the village when approaching by main road from the west.

10

Charing to Canterbury 15 miles

Charing

Charing was a place of some importance, for it possessed the greatest of those archiepiscopal palaces, the
string of which we came on first at Otford, and it was
also the last convenient halting-place for those pilgrims on the journey to Canterbury.

The archbishop's palace was built by Archbishop
John Stratford (1333–48), although little of the once
considerable establishment now remains standing.
Beside the approach road to the church from the
village street are the fourteenth-century gatehouse
and porter's lodge, and a range of domestic buildings
now converted into cottages in one block. Behind this
range was an irregular courtyard, now the farmyard,
which contained on the north side the residential
portion of the palace, now represented by the farmhouse. The once imposing fourteenth-century Great
Hall to the east has become a barn. On the north side
of the main block was the chapel, some traces of the
undercroft remain, whilst elsewhere round the perimeter of the grounds are traces of the original boundary walling.

The Great Hall must have been the scene of lavish
hospitality in its day. It is known that Henry VII was
entertained here by Archbishop Wareham on 24 March
1507, and Wareham was also host to Henry VIII, who

rested here one night when on his way to the Field of
the Cloth of Gold. The palace remained in possession
of the See of Canterbury until Cranmer resigned and
handed it over to Henry VIII. The palace stayed in
the hands of the Crown until the reign of Charles I,
and in 1692 the Manor was granted to the Wheeler
family, to whom it still belongs.

The Church of St Peter and St Paul dates from the
middle thirteenth-century, though there may have
been an earlier church on this site. The fine fifteenth-
century tower is built in the characteristic Kentish
Perpendicular style; square, with angle buttresses and
beacon turret. There is an embattled porch with a
vaulted roof dating from the same period. The nave
and other parts of the fabric were seriously damaged
by a fire in 1590, and the present nave roof, a magnificent and lofty span, with painted oak beams on fine
carved brackets, dates from 1592. The ornamental
roof in the chancel was built in 1620.

The church once possessed the block upon which
St John the Baptist lost his head. This much-revered
relic was brought back by Richard Coeur de Lion and
presented to the archbishops of Canterbury, but it
was removed by the Dissolution. In the vestry is
preserved a rare musical instrument, the long trumpet
or vamping horn, through which a loud humming
noise was made to accompany the orchestras of the
seventeenth and eighteenth centuries. Only six are
now in existence—five in England and one in
Germany.

Charing to Eastwell 4 miles

At Charing the great chalk hills turn a corner, where
the River Great Stour passes through a wide gap on
its way to Canterbury. Although the Downs continue
their general line above Wye to the Channel Coast at
Folkestone, we have reached the end of that long,

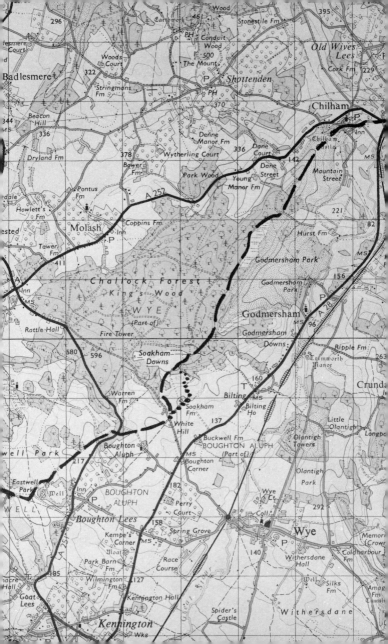

clean-cut ridge which we have followed all the way
from Farnham.

Beyond the crossing of A252 on Charing Hill the
Way is clearly marked by one of the KCC signs, and
once more we are on a clearly marked country lane
with banks on either side. The road continues for a
full mile as far as Burnthouse Farm, so named perhaps from its association with the adjacent limeworks.

Immediately beyond the farmhouse the track
bends sharply to the left and then to the right and we
come quite suddenly upon the limeworks hidden at
the edge of the wood. At the eastern end of the large
chalk pit, after 150 yards or so, the Way divides into
a fork. There is no KCC sign at this spot and it is easy
to take the wrong path. The right-hand one is the one
to follow, a rough track continuing at much the same
height as before, a terraceway bordered by trees and
bushes.

This is one of the most attractive spots along the
old road we have encountered since leaving the
wooded slopes above Boxley. The path runs through
a great beech wood, then we unexpectedly come
upon an ancient chalk working which is completely
overgrown and forms a deep coombe on the right. A
little way beyond, near height 426 feet, a road comes
up from the south and once more we are on a metalled highway which continues as far as Dunn Street,
where it runs into the road from Westwell to Challock.

From Dunn Street the old road enters Eastwell
Park and turns a gradual corner, following the course
of the Stour Valley. The modern road from Charing,
the A252, cuts off this corner and saves a good 2 or 3
miles to Chilham, but the reasons which caused men
to take the longer course are not easily overlooked:
1 The universal motive, the dryness of the road,
which could only be maintained upon the southern

side of the hills.

2 The slopes down to the Stour were open when the plateau above was dense forest, and this in turn would mean a group of villages, which are absent from the line of the main road.

3 The water supply of the plateau was stagnant and bad; that of the valley was a good running stream.

From Dunn Street the line of the Way is difficult to negotiate, for it passes through a long wood and is obstructed by many trees and much tangled undergrowth. Fortunately a well-established farm road runs parallel with it along the north edge of the wood. Leave the road, therefore, and curve left then right on a track past a large asbestos barn, then along the north edge of the wood to a railway level-crossing-type gate. At the next gate turn right through the wood, then left to the end of the wood. The line of the old road travels across three fields marked by tubular steel field gates, to reach the track to Walnut Tree Farm just north of Eastwell Church.

Eastwell

St Mary's Church now stands in ruins beside the edge of the lake. The roof of the church collapsed through neglect and war damage and pushed over the walls, leaving only the tower and some of the west wall standing.

The most imposing feature of the church was a great tomb with fine recumbent marble effigies and these are now protected by a brick and concrete cover. One of these would be the tomb of Sir Walter Moyle (died 1480), Earl of Winchilsea, and his wife, who lived at Eastwell House, while another is of Sir Thomas Moyle, speaker of the House of Commons, who rebuilt Eastwell House. Another tomb is reputed to be that of Richard Plantagenet, son of Richard III, who died in 1550. When the Plantagenets lost the day to the Tudors at the Battle of Bosworth Field and Richard III was killed, Richard, then aged 16, escaped and made his way into Kent in disguise. He worked as a mason and bricklayer on the Eastwell estate and when he died a record of his passing was made in the parish register and his body laid in the church. In his memory the well near Boughton Lees was later re-named Plantagenet's Well.

Eastwell Lake was formed in the park as part of the landscape improvements of the eighteenth century and covers some 40 acres. The whole of the park was under requisition by the army during the war and on the great lake Bailey bridges were tried out and troops trained in their use. After the war, during cleaning-up operations, a number of bicycles were fished out of the lake and the previously unexplained fate of the many bicycles reported missing after dark from the streets of Ashford was made abundantly clear!

The grounds of Eastwell were enclosed in the reign of Elizabeth I, and it may well be this act which caused the old road to fall into disuse and so account for the present doubt as to its original line. It is worth noting that no part of the old road is enclosed for so great a length as that which passes through Eastwell Park, where nearly two miles lie within the fence of a private owner.

The first house was built in Eastwell Park in the middle of the sixteenth-century, but on several occasions the mansion has been altered or rebuilt. The ninth Earl of Winchilsea demolished and rebuilt between 1793 and 1799 and again rebuilt in 1825. The property remained in the hands of the Earls of Winchilsea until 1900 and on the change of ownership the mansion was once more demolished and rebuilt, as we see it today, in imitation of the Tudor style.

Eastwell Park

Eastwell Park to Soakham Downs 2 miles

The line of the Pilgrims' Way is lost after Eastwell
church, but after a distance of about 2 miles the line
is recovered above the valley of the Stour on Soakham Downs. There are two possible routes between
these points and these must be examined before we
can proceed.

1 Through Boughton Lees and Boughton Aulph to Soakham Farm

This is the route favoured by the Kent CC. The
supposed line runs from Eastwell church along a road
lined with poplar trees to emerge at a lodge beside the
main road A251 in Boughton Lees. Here it turns a
right-angle, squarely to the left, along the road on the
east side of the village green to a cross-roads. Take the
road straight ahead leading to Boughton Aulph, KCC
signpost, and after nearly ½ mile a faded painted sign
points along a footpath between some orchard trees
to just south of Boughton Aulph church. This path
then continues across fields to White Hill at a road
leading to Wye. Here, just south of a quarry, is another KCC sign at the entrance of the track to Soakham Farm.

2 Through Eastwell Park, above Boughton Aulph to Soakham Farm

From Eastwell church the old road may have taken a
slightly higher line diagonally across the field to the
left of the road to pass in front of the mansion, then
along an avenue of beech trees where there is an
existing 'surfaced' park road to join the A251 Ashford
-Faversham highway at a sharp bend in the road.
There is a rough by-way leading almost due east from
a house beside the A251, and if this line is continued
across the re-entrant coombe below Warren Farm it
will strike the Wye road below the quarry at White
Hill.

In some respects this latter is the more convincing

Eastwell Park Lodge

alignment for Boughton Aulph church, like many others we have found, is passed to the north rather than to the south as the former line would make it do.

Warren Farm and Soakham Farm lie in deep coombes, while the lane from Wye to Challock and the main road A251 run up projecting spurs. We have found that when the old road came to obstacles of this kind it made for the neck of the promomtory and cut off the detour by passing just north of the crest, but at Soakham Farm the track turns straight up the hill, as a diagonal approach is not possible.

Just beyond Soakham Farm curve with the track along the edge of a field to an old sign beside a sheep dip. A yew tree marks the ascent up a steep and deeply cut gully lined with beech trees, and this curves up the hillside to the edge of a wood, which it enters. The footpath, however, keeps to the edge of the field then enters the wood to join the old road leading up to the crest of the Downs.

Perhaps the real explanation for these two routes is to be found in the crossing of the River Stour by ford, prior to the building of a bridge at Wye. Wye lay on an ancient and busy route along the Downs to the Channel ports, continuing the south-easterly course we have been following from the Medway and Stour crossings through Wye, Bradbourne and Monks Horton to reach the coast near Folkestone and Dover. Obviously travellers on this important trackway from the west to the coast would have sought the crossing of the Stour via Boughton Lees and Kempe's Corner; those who were bound for Canterbury would have kept more to the north above Boughton Aulph to Soakham Downs.

But why should there be alternative routes on this Canterbury diversion? Perhaps strangers from the west might have found a road junction at Eastwell, but, lacking guidance, followed a more prominent

southern course intended for those making for Wye.
On having reached Boughton Lees and the lower level
they would have discovered their mistake and so be
forced to take the obvious line back to the downland
crest—through Boughton Aulph.

It must not be forgotten that the traffic was not
all from west to east. One making the journey from
Canterbury with the object of crossing the Stour at
Wye for some destination to the south-west would
have followed the old road down to Soakham Farm
and then turned off for the ford. Those continuing
west towards Charing would keep on the higher level
above Boughton Aulph.

All evidence points therefore to the choice of the
higher-level route; it is more direct, avoids any sharp
bends, avoids unnecessary descent and ascent and
passes north of the church.

Soakham Downs to Chilham 3 miles

As we have seen before, the road does not take to the
crest of a hill without good reason, but once there it
often remains, especially if there is a spur upon which
it can fall gently down to the lower levels, in this case
straight to Chilham.

At the top of the wood above Soakham Farm the
Way keeps just on the edge of a big meadow on Soakham Downs and turns east to a gate. Here we enter a
very considerable area of forest, some 5,000 acres,
formerly known as King's Wood and now renamed
the 'State Forest of Challock'. One hundred yards
after the fire warning sign at the gate fork left at a
KCC sign and then, a little further on at the crossing
of a broad forestry road coming in from the left,
carry straight ahead, slightly downhill. After 100
yards, by a fire warning sign at a fork, bear up the
left-hand path, soon gaining the ridge where there are
views down over Godmersham Park.

The view across Godmersham Park is one of great beauty, with the Georgian mansion embowered in the trees below the great sweep of the Downs. The house was built in 1732 in a refined and consciously design-ed landscape by one Thomas Brodnax, who had changed his name first to May and then to Knight. His son, being childless, adopted a distant cousin, Edward Austen, as heir. Edward changed his name to Knight and eventually inherited the house, and when his wife died his sister sometimes came to stay and keep house for him. Her name was Jane Austen, whom we have already met, and the society she discovered here fascinated her and provided raw material for her novels.

Godmersham church stands near the bridge over the Stour beside the main valley road A28. On the south wall of the choir is a remarkable twelfth-century bas-relief of St Thomas Becket vested as archbishop with mitre and crook. This is the earliest known sculpture of the martyr and the only image known to have survived the efficient destruction of the Reformation.

The Pilgrims' Way leads through the woods for almost two miles along the heights above Godmer-sham Park. After the first mile the ground becomes open and cleared on the right and you may get occasional glimpses of Canterbury Cathedral through the trees. Just on the right over the old wooden fence can be seen traces of the old road. After a further ½ mile a forestry road comes up from the left, and on the right is a faded painted Pilgrims' Way sign. After another ½ mile the track bears right down to Hurst Farm and leaves the forest by a fire warning sign.

Continue ahead on a footpath and after a few hundred yards reach another footpath which crosses the hillside from Dane Street on the north to the ford across the Stour south of Hurst Farm. This crossing is marked by a stile in a fence spread around a thin

plantation on the site of an Iron Age settlement.
When he reaches this point the traveller is at a loss
how to proceed. There is very little trace of the
further course of the Way, but the woodland ride
ahead is an easily recognisable landmark. Continue
ahead between wire mesh fences through the plantation to reach a wide grassy ride at a corner. The
oldest and largest heronry in England is in Chilham
Park, and this may be found situated in many large
beech trees on the left-hand side of the ride leading
down to the right. Continue ahead down the ride,
which becomes a track through a wood, to reach a
gate and the edge of open ground of Chilham Park.

To reach Chilham village without trespassing on
private property it is necessary to retrace our steps to
the thin plantation on the site of the Iron Age settlement and continue down the woodland track towards
Hurst Farm, then turn along the road to Mountain
Street and so into Chilham.

Chilham

From whichever side you enter the village you will
climb up past old doorways and gables with projecting windows to emerge into a diminutive gravelled
square. On the two long sides are more of these old
houses and shops of contrasting styles and periods
forming a continuous facade. They are built in half-
timber and plaster, brick and stone, and have tiled
roofs; most are without front gardens, but some have
unfenced flower strips. All the views out of the village
square are closed, but note the surprising axial arrangement of the castle and the church, both seen among
trees through gaps at the ends of the square. The
blending and composition of materials, styles and
proportions makes Chilham a masterpiece of uncon-
scious planning.

Chilham claims to be the prettiest village in Kent

and the full horror of this claim may be realised on any Sunday afternoon in the summer, when the village square is choked with traffic and the clicking of camera shutters is deafening. Those residents who derive no commercial benefit from this invasion must curse those who have popularised this lovely village among the hop fields and orchards of Kent.

The fifteenth-century Perpendicular style Church of St Mary's stands at the east end of the square, with its low embattled flint and stone chequered tower reaching through the trees. There is a porch with a parvis, or upper chamber, and up near the roof of the nave are some excellent carvings.

The church is notable for its monuments, all of interest and some of quality, mainly to the Digges family, formerly residents of the castle. Those of Margaret, Lady Palmer (died 1619: north aisle) and Ez. Fogg (1626: south chapel) have arabesque and diaper patterns incised in the marble. The monument

in the south chapel to Sir Dudley Digges (1631) shows the four virtues: Justice, Prudence, Temperance and Fortitude. In the north chapel is a sculpture of 1822 to James Wildman and a sentimental memorial to the Hardy children (1858) showing the children with their toys. The fifteenth-century sarcophagus of Purbeck marble here was long thought to contain the remains of St Augustine, whose shrine was brought to the church after the dissolution of St Augustine's Abbey at Canterbury, but when it was opened in 1948 it was found to be empty.

At the west end of the square are the gates to Chilham Castle, home of the Viscount Massereene and Ferrard, DL. The 300-acre park is private property, but when the castle and gardens are open to the public—Wednesday, Thursday and Sunday afternoons from 1 May to 31 October and all Bank Holidays—we may walk through the mile-long park to search for the line of the old road.

Chilham Park is heavily timbered and proper identification of the old road in this section is most misleading. It is fairly likely, however, that the old road ran straight down the centre of the ridge in a direct line towards the castle. For the last few hundred yards the centre of the saddleback is all open ground. Beyond rise the grey walls of the ancient castle among the trees, while close by the mellow brickwork of the stately mansion shows richly colourful above the green lawn and the terraced and topiary gardens which were designed by 'Capability' Brown. Here were planted the first mulberry and wisteria in Britain, while in the park is a mile-long avenue of Spanish chestnuts and the oldest and largest heronry in England.

That the Romans established a station at Chilham and an important trackway passed immediately through, or near the site, seems to suggest that its choice as a defensive position must date far back into

The Square, Chilham

The Black Prince's Well, Harbledown

history. Commanding as it does the eastern end of the
great Wye Gap, the break in the Downs through
which the Stour finds outlet to the sea, such a choice
was an obvious one. It is reasonably safe to assume
therefore that the late Bronze Age people had a hill
fort here on the site of which the Romans established
a station, later converted by the Saxons for their own
use.

The massive octagonal keep which survives today
dates from the middle twelfth century. This is enclosed by a fourteenth-century curtain wall to form a
more or less rectangular bailey, but raised upon
twelfth-century foundations. On the north-east side
of the keep is an annexe, which when excavated in
1926 was discovered to be the remains of an eleventh-
century dungeon, containing fifteen skeletons.

The owners of Chilham had varying misfortunes.
John, Earl of Athol, was unfortunate enough to be
rashly involved in the Scottish wars against Edward I
and as a result paid the penalty with his life. His
successor, Bartholomew of Badlesmere, for refusing
Queen Isobel, consort of Edward II, entry to his
castle of Leeds (near Maidstone), met a similar fate.
Then Thomas, Lord Roos, having backed the House
of Lancaster in the Wars of the Roses, had his property seized by the Crown. Later Henry VIII granted
the estate to Sir Thomas Cheney, who proceeded to
demolish as much of the castle as he could to rebuild
his new mansion on the Isle of Sheppey. The remains
were purchased by Sir Thomas Kempe and in due
course his estates passed through inheritance to one
of his daughters, who was wife of Sir Dudley Digges.

Sir Dudley Digges was James I's Master of the
Rolls and he commissioned Inigo Jones to rebuild the
mansion, a brick Jacobean house which was completed in 1616. Like so many of its time the building
tries to reconcile the English Gothic tradition with
Renaissance ideas of classical design, with pleasingly

homely results. The design is on a revolutionary plan
illustrating the mathematical fancies of the age—a
regular hexagon with one side omitted. Above the
door is the inscription 'Dudley Digges AD 1616 Mary
Kempe', together with the pious phrase 'The Lord is
my house of defence and my castle'. In this house
was born Edward Digges, who became the Governor
of Virginia in 1655—8.

It is now impossible to determine exactly how the
line of the old road continued after passing the keep,
for the building of the house and the creation of the
terraced gardens has obliterated all the evidence.
Probably it passed to the north of the house to the
present village square, for here travellers, arriving too
late in the day to complete the journey to Canterbury, would have found welcome rest and refreshment.

Chilham to Canterbury 6 miles

Much uncertainty exists as to how the Way continued
from Chilham to Bigbury, and for the first 2 miles,
until the crossing of the London-Canterbury-Dover
railway line, the line is almost lost.

There is a tradition that the pilgrims of the later
Middle Ages passed down Church Hill—the lane
leading out of Chilham square on the north-west side
of the churchyard—crossed the Maidstone-Canterbury
road A252 in the valley below and ascended the
opposite hillside by a lane to the hamlet of Old Wives
Lees. This is the diversion favoured by the KCC, for
the road is signposted at the A252 junction in Chilham, in Old Wives Lees, and again on the A28 near
Shalmsford Street.

The pilgrims may have made the detour for the
purpose of visiting some special shrine or for some
other reason (as they did at Compton), but the route
turns a sharp corner to cross the damp and northern

side of a loamy hill in so doing. The known path
before Chilham goes south of the castle mound and
this would lead through the square and south of the
church, down the lane to the 'Woolpack' and so over
the southern shoulder of the hill towards Shalmsford
Street. The inn would seem to bear a significant
name, although when it was first so called is doubtful;
traditionally it is said to have been the home of the
master-builder employed by Sir Dudley Digges on his
mansion.

Cultivation and extensive road widening of the
present highway has swept away all traces of the old
road where it continues round the steep bank on the
curve to Whitehill. Bygone travellers, taking the line
of least resistance, would have kept below this high
bank rather than attempt to climb its steep side. At
this point there is a group of old cottages, and a back
lane running in the direction of Shalmsford Street
continues the line. One old name for this was 'Pikey
Lane' (piker = a tramp), suggesting that local tradition associated it with travellers, and it is now known
as 'Pilgrims' Lane'. An obvious depression in the lawn
of a house garden situated immediately opposite the
commencement of Pilgrims' Lane is on the same
alignment, and a series of tests have proved that
below the surface of the depression, which is about
10 feet wide, lay the surface of a forgotten road. At
the far end of Pilgrims' Lane we join the road leading
down from Old Wives Lees and then there are a few
fields before Shalmsford Manor is reached; but
immediately beyond the manor-house garden where
the ground rises there are unmistakable signs of an
old cart track again.

This spot, close to the river, must have been one of
considerable importance, for hard against the bridge
is the ford which provides the place-name in 'Shalmsford Street'. It is reasonable to assume that the ford
was used a great deal in medieval times by travellers

bound towards the Channel coast and possibly as an
alternative route towards Canterbury through Chartham. In 1908 a find made near some cottages in
Shalmsford Street would seem to indicate some
pilgrim traffic south of the Great Stour, for the
object discovered has been identified at the Canterbury Museum as a brass matrix of the seal of the Prior
of the Order of Hermit Friars of St Augustine's
Winchester, dated about 1480.

At Shalmsford Street the present highway A28
coincides with the old road for 600 yards or so beyond
the manor house to where the road makes a neat
right-angled bend within a few yards of the river. On
the left-hand side is a tall and very steep bank along
the base of which the Great Stour must have once
flowed. Any margin of level ground at this point
would have been marshy or liable to flooding, a most
unlikely place for a track to have been established,
particularly when a dry and easy path could have
been found on the higher ground above.

In actual fact, beyond the strip of orchard land
which runs in a north-easterly direction from a house
garden a short distance back, there seems to be an
obvious terraceway immediately below a grass-
covered bank some 100 feet above the level of the
river. This crosses the face of the hillside in the
direction of Nickle Farm, where a rounded spur of
the hill drops into a shallow orchard-clad valley
before the high railway embankment and the farm is
reached. If the Way crossed this land all traces of it
have been obliterated by cultivation, and the construction of the railway embankment adds to the
difficulty of identifying any sort of continuous line.
However, the lane leading from the main highway to
Nickle Farm passes through a brick archway in the
railway embankment and this was almost certainly
built to preserve the ancient approach. It seems
significant that the short length of road beyond the

railway arch lies in the same line as Shalmsford Manor; the railway arch must stand over the route of the old road. Just beyond the arch the lane comes to a dead end at the junction with several farm tracks. The one going east climbs the hillside to the edge of Fright Wood. It is deeply sunken and has every appearance of great antiquity. It is signposted at the start by an old timber sign 'Pilgrims' Way'.

At the top of the climb a concrete road is reached and 100 yards or so beyond are two old, lone dwellings called 'Puddledock Cottages', now modernised and picturesque in their quiet seclusion among the apple trees. The significance of their name becomes understandable when we approach the spot and find some springs which rise here below the wood. Immediately to the east the track forks and we continue the natural line along the northern reach to Hatch House and a gate, and when it emerges on the highway we find the KCC nameplate.

Here we enter the hamlet of Chartham Hatch and we continue up the road curving right along Town Lane to a road junction. Cross the junction along Bigberry Road (note the incorrect spelling) past an assortment of builder's allsorts ribboning out along the straight and level road to the eastern edge of the ridge where the road cuts right through the earthwork of Bigbury Camp, the last and the greatest of the prehistoric remains upon the line of the old road.

Bigbury Camp

The remains at Bigbury are a typical example of an early Iron Age hill fort, most likely thrown up against the attacks of the Belgae, invaders from northern France who managed to settle in Kent in the first-century. The lines of the camp are not easy to trace on the ground, being so much obscured by woodland undergrowth, old gravel workings and houses.

The camp occupies the eastern extremity of a gravel-capped spur some 250 feet high. It is almost 25 acres in extent, of irregular polygon shape with entrances at both east and west ends. The Way passes through the western one, but appears to have left the camp at a point somewhere south of the east gate. The road to Harbledown uses the east gate, and where there is a very sharp 'S' bend and a steep drop the defences, consisting of two deep ditches, can be seen quite clearly. The two high earthen banks separated by a deep ditch which formed the defensive ring can be traced nearly all round the perimeter of the camp, but cultivation has severely cut into them on the southern side. The banks were probably faced · with a timber stockade, for no trace of stone walls have been found.

Bigbury was the scene of Caesar's victory over the native forces which opposed his second landing in Kent in 54 BC. Caesar landed on the Channel coast somewhere between Thanet and Walmer. Following a night march inland of about 12 miles the Roman troops came upon the chariots and cavalry of the defenders advancing to meet them from some high land across a river, the Great Stour, perhaps near Tonford.

The numerous relics belonging to the pre-Roman people who occupied this important stronghold were mainly found in the gravel workings between 1861 and 1895. These include pottery objects and a few weapons, but principally they were iron agricultural tools; sickles, plough-shares, a plough coulter, and hammers and chisels. There was also a good deal of horse and chariot gear, equipment used for cooking, such as pot hooks and tripods, and slave collars and chains. Many of these finds are now in the Canterbury and Maidstone Museums.

Bigbury to Canterbury 2 miles

The Pilgrim's Way took the left-hand fork past Bigbury Camp in the direction of Harbledown, but a few
yards after the 'Z Bend' road sign it strikes across the
garden of 'Woodside' to reach the Tonford road by a
deep cutting. The true route of the old road cannot
be followed, so we must take the right-hand fork,
signposted by the KCC, past Bigbury Farm to the
Tonford road. Here we will find that the continuation
of the track is not immediately opposite but a few
yards up the road to the left, where there is a KCC
sign again.

On the east side of the Tonford road it will be
found that the signposted path is not actually the
Way itself but a modern route running parallel to it
for a few hundred yards and a few feet on its northern side. This has come into being because the old
road, here part terraceway and part sunken, is completely overgrown and it is impossible to walk the
original line. There is an orchard and a wire link fence
on the left and a belt of trees on the right, and when
these trees end and there are orchards on both sides
the path becomes deeply sunken between banks lined
with forest trees, an imposing woodland walk. The
Way then breaks into open country of a fertile valley,
with another apple orchard on the right and a hop
garden bordered by a wind-break of young poplars on
the left.

We have been descending the ridge from Bigbury
Camp to the valley in which the small Cranbourne
stream meanders on its course to the Great Stour.
The old road once crossed this brook by a ford, but
today a footbridge has been provided for the modern
traveller. I have been reluctant to advocate too many
detours from the Way itself, but at this point it is
obviously convenient to break the journey in order to
visit the village of Harbledown.

It is possible that some pilgrims after leaving

Bigbury Camp took the northern fork to join the A2
Watling Street near Harbledown, and then turned east
with the main throng from Chatham. The Watling
Street on its way eastwards crosses a series of ridges,
and the village of Harbledown was nicknamed 'Bob-
up-and-down', recorded by Chaucer in 'The Manciple's
Tale' Prologue as

'a litel town
Which that ycleped is Bob-up-and-down
Under the Blee in Canterbury Way '

Harbledown

Leave the Way at the footbridge over the Cranbourne
stream and walk along the farm road following the
stream and leading to the village, passing through hop
fields and alongside big farm buildings and hop oasts.

Just before reaching the main road go by a path on
the right leading up to the almshouses, and at the
beginning of the ascent you will come to the famous
spring the 'Black Prince's Well' or the 'Well of St
Thomas'. The spring is surrounded by a brick kerb and
half enclosed by a niche of ancient masonry partly
built into the hillside, an unexpected and charming
setting. In the old days the water from this font was
thought to possess healing virtues, being considered
to be good for the treatment of eye diseases and
leprosy. It is told that the Black Prince drank here on
his last journey from Canterbury to London, while
another tells that the Prince was lying on his death-
bed at Westminster when he craved for some water
from the well at Harbledown.

The path leads up to the almshouses established in
1840 on the site of a leper hospital founded by
Lanfranc in 1084. The supply of lepers soon dimini-
shed and the foundation became first a hospital for
ordinary diseases and then a home for the aged. As
part of his penance for his uttering the words that

brought about Becket's death, Henry II in 1174 made a grant in perpetuity to this hospital of 40 marks, this sum to be deducted from money due to him from Canterbury and paid by the city annually on his behalf. Even today the yearly sum of £13.33½ (one Henry II mark now being worth 33½) is still paid to the hospital by the City Treasury, thus ensuring continuance of a royal grant made nearly 800 years ago.

Did the name Harbledown come from 'herbal down', simple medicines extracted from herbs for the hospital patients? Many interesting relics are preserved in the hall of this quiet retreat, one of them being a small turned money box guarded by an attached chain. According to tradition this is the actual box that the Dutchman Erasmus, when he passed this way with his friend John Colet about 1512, dropped a coin into after refusing on hygienic grounds the request of a leper inmate to kiss what was claimed to be a crystal from the shoe of Archbishop Becket.

Standing above the almshouses is the Norman Church of St Nicholas, having a wonderful view of Canterbury Cathedral. The church has much of interest, including benches on which lepers sat, and also a sloping floor which facilitated washing down the tiles after each service attended by those afflicted.

The view of the Cathedral from this point must have delighted all the pilgrims after their long and arduous journey. St Thomas's shadow has lain over the whole of this road and as we descend the hill to Canterbury our hearts are lifted as we near our goal.

Approach to Canterbury

From the Cranbourne stream the old road ascends steeply by an attractive woodland path. Halfway up this path the Way has been diverted and on the right can be seen a sunken lane of the original line. Near

the top this rejoins the path and from the deep tun-
nelled shade of the trees we suddenly emerge upon an
appalling new housing estate spreading over the
hillside. Golden Hill on the left is National Trust
property and was presented to them to preserve a
famous view of the Cathedral, but this has now
unfortunately been entirely blotted out by buildings
and trees.

From the top of Golden Hill the Way descends
through leafy Mill Lane, soon bordered by houses and
after ¼ mile leads into the A2 London Road, formerly Watling Street. It was at this spot that travellers
and pilgrims who had followed the Downland trackway as we have done joined the bigger company from
London. Arriving at this spot on a summer's evening
they would see the towers of the majestic Cathedral
shining golden in the sun above the old red roofs of
the city.

Cross over the dual carriageway of the A2 and
continue straight along London Road to the A290
Canterbury-Whitstable road, turning sharp right by
the church of St Dunstan-Without-the-Westgate.
We have seen that the old road never turns a sharp
corner, but only here and at Winchester does it break
this rule. It had to do so here because the Way has
been following a course upon the north bank of the
Stour, the opposite bank from that upon which
Canterbury grew: a ferry or bridge had to be provided
across the river and this would necessarily turn at a
right-angle from a path upon the opposite bank.

A window in the west wall of the chancel chapel
of St Dunstan's shows Dunstan, Sir Thomas More
and Lanfranc, and from the top of the tower can be
obtained a grand view of the city. On the opposite
side of St Dunstan's Street can be seen the Roper
Gateway, a red-brick Tudor building now part of a
brewery. Margaret Roper, daughter of Sir Thomas
More, Lord Chancellor of England, lived here for a

time. When her father lost his head on 6 July 1535
because of his steadfast opposition to the divorce of
Henry VIII from Queen Katherine of Aragon, Margaret Roper was rowed up the Thames to below London Bridge, where a friend threw down the head from
the spear upon which it was exhibited. She carried
her precious relic to Harbledown and it was interred
in the church of St Nicholas, but now it is resting in
St Dunstan's in a lead casket.

Continue down St Dunstan's Street, cross the
bridge over the Stour and enter the city proper under
West Gate, the only survivor of the six medieval gates
in the city walls. The gateway was rebuilt in 1380,
but the massive twin towers have witnessed many
memorable scenes before and after that date. Henry
II came this way 'barefoot and weeping' on 12 July
1174 after changing into the garb of penitence at St
Dunstan's Church to seek atonement at the shrine of
St Thomas for his grim deed. In 1189 came Richard
Coeur de Lion with William the Lion, King of Scotland, but in 1376 was probably the most impressive
event of all—the funeral cortege of the Black Prince,
eldest son of Edward III and victor of the battles of
Crecy and Poitiers. The body of this national hero
was brought to its resting-place in the Trinity Chapel
of the Cathedral with all the splendour that medieval
pomp could provide; the processions of Henry V on
his way to Agincourt, Charles Stuart and Oliver
Cromwell were dull in comparison.

From about 1400 the West Gate was the city
prison, from which prisoners walked out only to the
gallows. It is today a museum of arms and armour
and a nuisance to traffic, but an indispensable trea-
sure to Canterbury nevertheless. The general view of
the city and the Cathedral from the roof of the gate is
one of the most impressive of any cathedral city.

The West Gate is built over one reach of the Stour
and we enter St Peter's Street, which at first sight

appears as a modern town planner's nightmare and a historian's delight—a higgledy-piggledy of all building styles and frontages, where windows and overhanging upper storeys jut and butt out over the narrow pavements. This is part of the fascination we expect of Canterbury, old mellow-fronted shops and ancient buildings jostling with the new.

At King's Bridge there are the self-consciously picturesque weavers houses of Flemish refugees by the side of another branch of the Stour. Across the road astride the river is the Hospital of St Thomas the Martyr upon Eastbridge, founded in 1175 to provide beds for poor pilgrims who came to pray at the Shrine of the Martyr in the Cathedral. Later it became a hospital, with a chapel used as a school, and now it is partly a museum and open to the public.

High Street follows next, and soon on the left we come to narrow Mercery Lane. In this street were situated the inns which provided rest and refreshment for the medieval pilgrims, and shops and stalls where the pilgrims could buy healing water from Becket's Well in the cathedral crypt, medallions of St Thomas and other tokens of their pilgrimage. The overhanging fronts of the shops in the narrow lane still convey the medieval atmosphere, and souvenirs are sold to the modern tourist much as they were several centuries ago.

At the far end of the lane is the quaint little square of the Butter Market outside the great Christchurch Gateway. This magnificent and elaborate gateway was built in 1517-20 and has wooden doors dating from 1662. It is decorated with painted heraldic shields and is one of the most beautiful specimens of Perpendicular work in the country. The two turrets of the gate are recent additions. The originals were taken down in the eighteenth century to please people living at a distance who said they obstructed their view of the cathedral clock!

11 Canterbury

On entering Canterbury Cathedral it is advisable to sit down for a short time to allow the eyes and mind to become accustomed to their surroundings. The Cathedral Church of Christ at once casts the spell of its beautiful proportions, the vastness of the interior, the dazzling splendour of its glowing stained glass, its tomb with effigies lying in age-old peace. We arrive at the north-west transept and linger at the scene of the martyrdom and the steps worn thin by the countless pilgrims before us. A slab of stone set into the east wall marks the spot near which Becket is supposed to have fallen.

Your mind is alive with visions of the past that even the milling throng of package-tour sightseers cannot blot out. You can imagine the hard face of Becket in profile gazing fixedly, still caught by the last rays of twilight filtering through the windows high up on the southern side; the choir beyond chanting; the battering of the oak door; the jangle of arms and of scabbards trailing as the four knights broke in—William de Tracy, Hugh de Morville, Reginald Fitzurse and Richard le Breton; the exchange of sharp and angry insults; the blows, then Gilbert groaning, wounded, and Becket dead. The Cathedral is silent and empty, an awful and fitting terminal to the long journey.

The murder of St Thomas and the pilgrimages that followed formed only a comparatively late page in

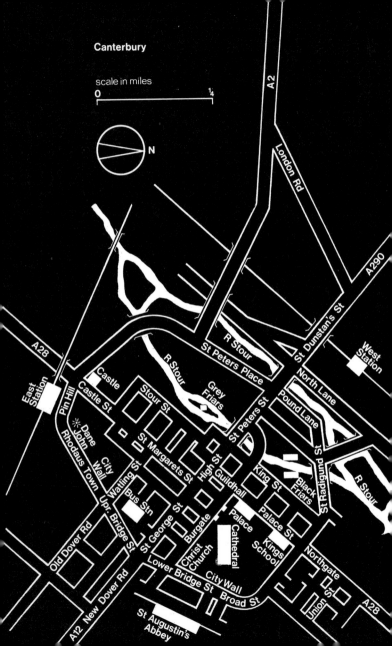

the religious history of Canterbury, for this city was the birthplace of Christianity in England and is the chief cathedral city in the kingdom, its archbishop bearing the title of Primate of All England.

About AD 590 the town became the capital of King Ethelbert, the fourth Saxon king of Kent and a heathen. His queen, Bertha, a French princess, was already a Christian when she arrived in Kent, and in her marriage agreement it had been stipulated that she should be allowed to practise her religion in her husband's kingdom. Ethelbert allocated a Roman building for her use as a Christian church, and this, St Martin's Church of Canterbury, can therefore claim to be the oldest church in England. It contains a font which is almost certainly the one where King Ethelbert was baptised by St Augustine on his eventual conversion on Whit Sunday in 597.

Under the influence of his queen, Ethelbert welcomed St Augustine and his forty fellow missionaries from Rome when they landed at Ebbsfleet in Thanet in 597. Augustine was given land by Ethelbert and established a Benedictine monastery, the church of which, St Peter and St Paul, became the burial place of the kings of Kent and the first archbishops. The extensive St Augustine's Abbey is now in ruins.

The city was laid waste by the Danes in the mid-ninth century and again in 1011, when Archbishop Alphege was martyred. The Cathdral of Christ Church was restored to its former dignity in 1023 by Canute, now a Christian, only to be destroyed by fire forty four years later, in 1067. It was rebuilt by Archbishop Lanfranc, the first Norman bishop in 1070, who also reorganised the monastery of Christ Church as a priory. The building was completed in seven years, but it proved quite inadequate for its purpose as cathedral and priory church, and in 1096 a reconstruction of the east end was planned by Lanfranc's successor, St Anselm (1093-1109). Begun under the

directions of Prior Ernulf (1096-1107), the work on this was continued on an even grander scale after 1107 by Prior Conrad (1108-26), who extended the building to nearly twice its previous size. The new church was consecrated in 1130 in the presence of the Kings of England and Scotland and all the English bishops.

Archbishop Becket was canonised in 1172 and the great numbers of pilgrims to his miracle-working tomb in the crypt determined that a more elaborate east end should be built as a fitting temple for the shrine of the saint. The saint's remains lay for fifty years in the eastern end of the crypt, a vast subterranean chapel, the largest and most elaborate in England, entered from the south-west transept.

The new shrine was built by a renowned French architect, William of Sens, who in 1175 began a splendid new choir, 191 feet long; and a presbytery, modelled on his previous work in the Cathedral of Sens, a mixture of Roman and Gothic but modified to suit the special considerations imposed by the surviving parts of Conrad's church. Stone for the building was brought from Caen in Normandy and landed at Fordwich, the point up to which the Stour was still navigable at that time. Crippled by a fall from the scaffolding, William continued to direct the work from his bed until the eastern transepts were finished in 1179. He then relinquished his task to another William, usually called William the Englishman to avoid confusion, who, working on the plans of French William, completed the Chapel of St Thomas (Trinity Chapel), the Corona, and the Crypt beneath them by 1184. In 1220 the remains of Becket were transfered with great pomp to the new shrine in the Trinity Chapel.

The twelve windows in the Trinity Chapel illustrate his life and death and the miracles he worked. At the top of the steps in the north aisle low down in the

Canterbury Cathedral. The Nave looking East

first window of twelfth-century glass is a frequently
missed depiction of Thomas Becket fully vested. At
the top of the fifth window the golden shrine on its
pillars is represented. Immediately behind St Augustine's Chair, in which he never sat, is the Corona or
Becket's Crown containing one of the Poor Man's
Bible windows in thirteenth-century glass.

For over 150 years the Cathedral remained un-
touched, then in 1378 Archbishop Simon of Sudbury
(1375-81) pulled down the Norman work which was
beyond repair and began a magnificent new nave and
transepts in the English Perpendicular style to the
designs of Henry Yevele, the master mason of Edward
III. The nave, 188 feet long, 72 feet wide and 80 feet
high, was completed about 1410 under Prior Chillen-
den (1390-1421). The south-west tower was rebuilt
by Thomas Mapildon for Archbishop Chichele about
1435, but Lanfranc's north-west tower stood until
1834, when it was replaced by an exact copy of
Chichele's tower, a matching pair both 178 feet high.
The central tower, the Bell Harry Tower, is 235 feet
high and was built by John Wastell in 1485-98. It is a
notable example of the Perpendicular style, with a
magnificent fan-vaulted lantern ceiling. Curfew is
rung nightly from Bell Harry, which takes its name
from a bell given by Prior Henry de Eastry. It may be
climbed by 287 steps. With a total length of 517 feet
Canterbury ranks as the fourth largest English cathedral. Winchester, the largest, is 556 feet long.

The pilgrimages were already on the decline when
Henry VIII destroyed the Shrine of St Thomas in
1538, and only the surrounding pavement of Italian
mocaic, worn into grooves by the toes and knees of
the pilgrims, remains to mark the site of the tomb.
So magnificently adorned was the shrine that in 1512
Erasmus wrote that 'gold was the meanest thing to be
seen'. The priory was dissolved in 1540 and the
affairs of the Cathedral placed under the jurisdiction

Canterbury Cathedral. The Choir facing East

of a Dean and Chapter. The Cathedral suffered during
the Civil War, when it was desecrated by the Puritan
fanatic Richard Culmer, one of the ministers appointed to destroy objects of idolatrous worship, but it
escaped the worse intentions of the German bombers
on June and October of 1942.

It is impossible to describe here all the buildings of
great antiquity and other places of interest that
abound in Canterbury, but we will inevitably set out
to enjoy the rich inheritance of the Pilgrims' City.

The overriding impression to the casual visitor is
of a city of sharp visual contrasts and no overall
unity. The main streets vary from an attractively
intimate scale with buildings and frontages of different periods and styles uniting into a harmonious and
picturesque streetscape to the clumsy monumentality
of the widened St George's Street with St George's
Tower standing forlornly among the unimaginative
urban designs of twentieth century-midland-
commercial development.

The growth of motor-vehicle ownership, together
with the changing conditions in social habits, have
meant that the town centre is not able to cope with
the recent dramatic change in pace. The town is
presented with problems that threaten to destroy or
at least greatly alter its character, and the resultant
effect of these pressures is reflected in the opening up
of precincts, the widening of streets and the infill of
new buildings, all of which are completely out of
scale and totally unsympathetic to the general streetscape of the town centre.

The enclosing city walls circle the narrow and
irregular streets of an almost unchanged medieval
street layout which are overflowing with the daily
increasing traffic. On Saturdays the main streets seize
up so completely that even the dodge of forming a
one-way system has ceased to be tolerable. Opposite

Canterbury Cathedral

the city walls at the Riding Gate the new fire station with its flint walls has been blended with the ancient stonework that is pleasing to the eye, but there are a few other instances where modern brickwork could have been tempered by a partial disguising to match buildings close by. In the Longmarket a modern tall building completely ruins a vista of the Cathedral from the High Street.

The old streets contain many buildings of interest, but also have many gaps and run-down houses under the threat of demolition. Any large sites left after demolition are used as temporary car parks, appalling and extensive vistas of tarmac occupying a considerable area of the historic core awaiting development. A multi-storey car park, grey and stark, said by some to be hideously ugly, others seeing it as beautiful, was opened in 1969. On the southern side of the city a primary distributor road built on the old moat opens up new views of the city walls for passing travellers.

It has been argued that to prevent the chaos of surface car parking and to justify a policy of restricted access in the city a multi-storey car park within the city walls is necessary and this, together with published road schemes which would involve the destruction of some of Canterbury's most remarkable assets, has raised many objections to the management of traffic in the city.

One third of the central area of Canterbury was laid in ruins during the war but little of historic value was destroyed. Many people moved out, and in the process of rebuilding remains of Roman houses and streets were discovered. The rebuilding set a pattern for large scale development in the centre, and vacant sites resulted in parking facilities being provided and taken for granted very close to the shops. Modern commercial pressures have been accepted as a basis for developing a thriving shopping centre in the heart of the city instead of preserving the city's best features and maintaining the environment.

Canterbury cannot survive simply as a musuem piece, but in addition to its traditional role as a tourist attraction it has another important function: to resist the modern commercial pressures by retaining its human scale and well-defined environment; quiet, relaxing, sharply divided from some of the less attractive features of modern city life. Once the distinctive atmosphere of small-scale old winding streets with their continuous frontages and the overall medieval character have gone, people may not come just to visit the historic buildings which remain.

In 1970, on the 800th year of Becket's death, a festival took place. Numerous religious and artistic events were presented jointly by the City of Canterbury and the Dean and Chapter of Canterbury Cathedral.

These included special services, music concerts and lectures in the cathedral. A regal and royal pilgrim was Her Majesty, Queen Elizabeth, the Queen Mother, who attended the National Service on 15 July, at which the Archbishop of Canterbury gave an address.

Also held was a Son et Lumiere—'Conflict at Canterbury'—with the physical presence of the cathedral as its background, T.S. Eliot's 'Murder in the Cathedral' staged inside the building for the first time ever, while a new Becket play, 'A Breach in the Wall', by Ray Lawdler, received its world premiere at the Marlow Theatre.

Don't leave your pilgrimage to Canterbury too late. At the present rate of 'comprehensive redevelopment' the 1970s will be commemorating the martyrdom of Canterbury as well.

Appendix

The North Downs Way

The North Downs Way, a 141-mile long distance footpath, received Ministerial approval on 14 July 1969,
but many miles of new rights of way are required to
complete it. Greatest progress has been made east of
the Medway Gap, but agreement for other stretches is
painfully slow. Until the new rights of way have been
negotiated the route will not exist as a public right
of way in its entirety, a problem shared by the present
Pilgrims' Way. Some official Countryside Commission
acorns have been displayed on agreed footpaths and
several of these will be seen when on the Pilgrims'
Way, as the two routes coincide for much of the
distance of the long-distance path.

The North Downs Way starts near Farnham railway station, on the A31 road, and follows and crosses
the River Wey before rising to higher ground north of
Crooksbury Hill, south of the Pilgrims' Way. Continuing eastwards it passes close to and south of the
village of Seale, and enters the village of Puttenham
by way of Puttenham Common. From here to St
Martha's Church the path follows the route of the
Pilgrims' Way, and it is proposed that the River Wey
be crossed by a new footbridge by St Catherine's.
East of St Martha's the path goes along Albury Downs.
by Newlands Corner at road A25, and then along the
escarpment through the woodlands at Netley Heath
to Ranmore Common, then down to cross the busy
A24 road north of Dorking by way of an existing

underpass, to the River Mole.

The North Downs Way crosses the River Mole by the stepping-stones, as does the Pilgrims' Way, ascends Box Hill and proceeds along the escarpment, joining the Pilgrims' Way again just beyond Pebble Coombe. The two routes are coincidental along the Buckland Hills, Colley and Reigate Hill through Gatton Park to Merstham. Here the path will pass under the proposed South Orbital Road, M25, just west of the A23 road, follow the A23 for 300 yards before continuing to White Hill, where it joins the route of the Pilgrims' Way again. The two routes pass over Gravelly Hill to road A22, which is being widened and where a new footbridge is proposed. For the remaining length to the county boundary at road B2024 the path will take the line of the Pilgrims' Way some way down the scarp slope, because the crest is followed by a road and there is a large quarry and lime works at Oxted and plantations at Botley Hill.

From the county boundary the path follows the mid-slopes of the hills above the Pilgrims' Way to Chevening Park, then to Dunton Green and across the valley of the Darent to Otford. It then ascends the hills and continues by field path through wooded country to Wrotham, there joining the Pilgrims' Way and following it as far as Whitehorse Wood. From here the long-distance path continues north-eastwards by Holly Hill to reach the Medway south of Rochester, where it crosses the river by the footbridge alongside the M2 motorway. It continues east of the Medway by Wouldham Downs and Bluebell Hill and on to Detling. From Detling the path runs at a higher level than the Pilgrims' Way, but descends slightly to join it at Hollingbourne and follows it all the way to Charing and Boughton Lees in the Great Stour valley.

From the Great Stour valley the North Downs Way runs from Wye and climbs the Downs again near Hastingleigh and proceeds along the crest with a further short descent to the village of Stowting; then to Etchinghill and by way of Cheriton Hill, Cherry Garden Hill, Castle Hill, Round Hill and Sugar Loaf Hill to the road A260 on the outskirts of Folkestone. From this road the path follows Cretway Down to the cliffs east of Folkestone, and then goes along the cliff tops to Dover. On those occasions when firing is taking place at the Lydden Spout ranges an alternative path is to be provided slightly inland.

The Canterbury Link branches from the main path at Boughton Lees in the Great Stour valley and ascends north-eastwards to Soakham Downs to join the route of the Pilgrims' Way, skirting Godmersham and Chilham Parks to Chilham, then through the orchard country to Harbledown and Canterbury East of Canterbury the path again traverses orchard country to Patrixbourne and then by Barham Downs to Shepherdswell, turning eastwards through Waldershare Park and then southwards by way of the Roman Road to Dover.

Author	Title	Publisher
Hilaire Belloc	The Old Road	Constable 1904
R.H. Goodsall	The Ancient Road to Canterbury	Constable 1960
Henry Fearon	The Pilgrimage to Canterbury	Associated Newspapers
Donald Maxwell	The Pilgrims' Way to Kent	Kent Messenger 1932
D.J. Hall	English Medieval Pilgrimages	Routledge & Kegan Paul 1966
N. Pevsner	Buildings of England Series	Penguin 1959
A. Mee	Kings England Series	Hodder & Stoughton 1936-1956
B.V. Fitzgerald	County Book Series	Robert Hale 1949
A.E. Trueman	Scenery of England & Wales	Gollancz 1938
J.F. Lousley	Wild Flowers of Chalk & Limestone	Collins 1950
Geoffrey Chaucer	The Canterbury Tales	
R.M.C. Anderson	The Roads of England	Ernest Benn 1932
W.A. Poucher	The Surrey Hills	Chapman & Hall 1949
Sean Jennett	The Pilgrims' Way	Cassell 1971
Ronald Hamilton	Summer Pilgrimage	P. & G. Wells Winchester 1973